MICROSOFT
POWERPOINT GUIDE

A Presentation Software

Copyright © 2013 John Monyjok Maluth

***

Discipleship Press

Website: www.discipleshippress.wordpress.com
Email: maluthabiel@gmail.com
Phone: +254 110 424 822

~~***~~

P.O. Box 28448-00100, Nairobi Kenya

Library of Congress Control Number: 2022907653

All rights reserved. No part of this book may be reproduced, stored in a retrieval system, or transmitted in any or by any means—electronic, mechanical, photocopying, recording, or otherwise-without prior permission in writing from the copyright holder.

CONTENTS

PART ONE: GET STARTED FAST 1

PART TWO: THE POWERPOINT WORKSPACE 17

PART THREE: BUILDING SLIDES THAT MAKE SENSE 40

PART FOUR: HOME TAB (THE DAILY TOOLS) 61

PART FIVE: INSERT TAB (MAKE SLIDES RICH, NOT BUSY) 82

PART SIX: DESIGN TAB (MAKE IT LOOK CLEAN AND CONSISTENT) 99

PART SEVEN: ANIMATIONS AND TRANSITIONS (USE WITH CONTROL) 115

PART EIGHT: SLIDE SHOW TAB (PRESENT LIKE A PRO) 136

PART NINE: REVIEW TAB (FIX, COLLABORATE, PROTECT) 153

PART TEN: VIEW TAB (WORK FASTER AND STAY ORGANIZED) ... 171

PART ELEVEN: OTHER HIDDEN TABS AND POWER FEATURES 192

PART TWELVE: KEY TERMINOLOGIES AND QUICK HELP 211

DISCLAIMER

Computer software changes, and some details in computer books can become outdated. The author and publisher have worked to keep this book accurate at the time of writing, but they cannot accept liability for errors, omissions, or results from using the information in this book. This guide is for education only and is not a substitute for professional advice. The author and publisher do not endorse any specific software or hardware mentioned here. Always test and confirm steps on your own computer before using them for work or important tasks.

HOW TO USE THIS GUIDE

This guide is written for beginners and practical users.

If you want quick results, read the introduction, learn the PowerPoint main window, then go straight to the Home tab and Insert tab. After that, use Design, Animations, and Slide Show to polish and present.

If you want full confidence, follow the chapters in order and practice on your computer as you read. Do not only read. Create a small presentation and keep improving it with each chapter.

When you see a feature you do not understand yet, do not panic. Continue reading. Many tools make more sense after you see them used in a real presentation.

PART ONE: GET STARTED FAST

This part is for the beginner who wants results today. You will learn what PowerPoint is, where it is used, what "versions" really mean, how to open it correctly, and how to build your first short presentation in about 10 minutes.

By the end of this part, you will be able to:

- open PowerPoint and choose the right starting option (blank, template, or recent)
- create a new presentation from scratch
- add three slides quickly
- write a clean title and simple bullet points
- save your file properly using a clear name and a reliable folder

If you do nothing else, do the mini project at the end. That small practice will teach you more than reading alone.

1) What PowerPoint Is (and Why People Use It)

Microsoft PowerPoint is a presentation program. It helps you communicate ideas using slides, not long pages of text.

A PowerPoint file is called a presentation. A presentation is made of slides. Each slide is like one page on your screen, but it is meant to be shown to people, usually on a projector, TV, or shared screen.

PowerPoint is used because it helps people:

- organize thoughts in a clear order

- teach step by step
- show pictures, charts, and tables
- keep attention by mixing words and visuals
- speak with confidence using speaker notes

PowerPoint is not only for big companies. It is for anyone who needs to explain something clearly.

Where PowerPoint Is Commonly Used

A) School and Education

PowerPoint is used in:

- classroom lessons
- student presentations
- project defenses
- seminars and workshops

Students use PowerPoint to summarize research, explain projects, and present findings. Teachers use it to guide lessons and keep learners focused.

B) Work and Business

PowerPoint is used in:

- meetings and briefings
- reports and updates
- product pitches
- staff training

- proposals and plans

In work settings, PowerPoint helps teams communicate quickly. Instead of reading a long report, people can see the key points on slides, then discuss the details.

C) Ministry and Church Work

PowerPoint is widely used in:

- sermons and teaching sessions
- Bible study lessons
- worship lyrics display
- announcements and church programs
- conferences and discipleship training

In ministry, PowerPoint helps people follow along. It also helps the speaker stay on track while sharing scripture references, key points, and visuals.

D) Training and Community Programs

PowerPoint is used in:

- health education and awareness sessions
- NGO trainings and workshops
- community mobilization events
- leadership and skills programs
- orientation sessions for new staff

Trainers like PowerPoint because it supports structured teaching. It also makes group learning easier, especially when the audience includes new learners.

What PowerPoint Is NOT

PowerPoint is not:

- a word processor like Microsoft Word
- a spreadsheet tool like Microsoft Excel
- a replacement for your speech

PowerPoint supports your message. It should not replace your message.

A good presenter does not read every word on the slide. The slide is the signpost. The speaker is the guide.

2) PowerPoint Versions: What Changes and What Stays the Same

You will hear people say "PowerPoint 2007," "PowerPoint 2010," "PowerPoint 2016," "PowerPoint 2021," or "Microsoft 365 PowerPoint." Those names refer to different versions.

A version is simply a release of the software. Over time, Microsoft updates PowerPoint by adding features, changing menus, and improving performance.

Here is the most important truth for beginners:

The Big Change Happened in 2007

PowerPoint 2007 introduced the Ribbon. The Ribbon is the tabbed menu at the top that contains commands such as Home, Insert, Design, and Slide Show.

If you learn PowerPoint 2007 and later, you are learning the modern style of PowerPoint. That is why many books focus on "PowerPoint 2007 and later."

What Stays the Same in PowerPoint 2007 and Later

Even when the design changes, these things stay the same:

- PowerPoint still uses slides
- you still add text, pictures, shapes, and charts
- you still use layouts and themes
- you still present using Slide Show mode
- you still save and share files
- the main tabs still exist (Home, Insert, Design, Transitions/Animations, Slide Show, Review, View)

So do not worry if your version looks slightly different from someone else's. The core skills are stable.

What Changes from Version to Version

These are common changes across versions:

- the start screen design (how the program looks when it opens)
- new templates and theme styles
- new visual features for smooth movement and modern effects
- better collaboration and sharing features
- improved media support (audio and video)

- new export options (like video export improvements)
- new tools for design help

Sometimes Microsoft moves a button to a different place. Sometimes an option is renamed. But the purpose of the tool stays the same.

A Simple Way to Think About Versions

Use this simple rule:

If you can find the Home tab and Insert tab, you can do most of your work.

When you change computers or use a newer PowerPoint, do not panic. Look for:

- the Ribbon at the top
- the tabs (Home, Insert, Design, etc.)
- the slide thumbnails on the left
- the main slide area in the center

If you can see those, you are ready.

3) Launching PowerPoint and Choosing a Starting Point

Opening PowerPoint is easy, but beginners often start in the wrong way. They open an old file by mistake. Or they click a template they do not understand. Or they start writing without saving.

This section teaches you a clean start.

A) How to Launch PowerPoint

On Windows

Common ways:

- Start Menu → type "PowerPoint" → press Enter
- click the PowerPoint shortcut on your desktop
- search from the taskbar search box and open PowerPoint

On Mac

Common ways:

- Applications folder → Microsoft PowerPoint
- Dock icon (if it is pinned)
- Spotlight search → type "PowerPoint"

On the Web

If you use the web version, you usually open it through your Microsoft account in a browser. The web version is useful for quick editing and sharing, but many beginners learn faster using the desktop app first.

B) The Start Screen: Three Safe Options

When PowerPoint opens, you usually see a start screen. It might show templates, recent files, and search boxes.

As a beginner, you have three safe options:

1. Blank Presentation
2. Template
3. Recent Files

Let's break them down.

Option 1: Blank Presentation

Use Blank Presentation when:

- you want full control
- you want to learn the tools
- you are creating a simple deck quickly

Blank Presentation is the best choice for your first practice.

Option 2: Template

A template is a ready-made design. It can help you create a beautiful presentation fast.

Use a template when:

- you want quick design without much formatting
- you are making a common type of deck (report, pitch, training, newsletter-style slides)

But beginners should be careful with templates. Some templates have many decorative shapes. They look nice, but they can confuse you while learning.

If you use a template, choose a simple one.

Option 3: Recent Files

Recent files are presentations you opened recently.

Use Recent Files when:

- you are continuing your work

- you know exactly which file you want

Do not click a recent file if you are not sure. You may edit the wrong document by mistake.

---

4) Your First Mini Project (10 Minutes)

This is your first real practice. Follow these steps slowly. Create the slides on your computer while reading.

Your goal: build a 3-slide presentation called "My First Presentation."

Before You Start: Create a Folder for Practice

A professional habit is to save files into a folder, not on the desktop without order.

Create a folder named:
PowerPoint Practice

Inside it, you can create another folder named:
My First Presentation

This habit will save you many headaches later.

Step 1: Create a New File

1. Open PowerPoint.
2. Choose Blank Presentation.
3. You should now see one slide, usually a Title Slide.

Keyboard shortcut (Windows):

- Press Ctrl + N to create a new presentation

If you already opened PowerPoint and it shows an old file, create a new one using:
File → New → Blank Presentation

Step 2: Add 3 Slides

You already have Slide 1 (Title Slide). Now you need Slide 2 and Slide 3.

1. Click the Home tab.
2. Click New Slide.

Do it twice so you have three slides total.

You will see slide thumbnails on the left side:

- Slide 1
- Slide 2
- Slide 3

Keyboard shortcut (Windows):

- Press Ctrl + M to add a new slide

Tip:
If New Slide creates a slide layout you do not want, click the small arrow under New Slide and choose a layout such as:

- Title and Content
- Section Header
- Two Content

For beginners, "Title and Content" is the easiest.

Step 3: Add a Title and Bullets

Now you will write simple text.

Slide 1: Title Slide

1. Click inside the title box.

2. Type:
   My First Presentation

3. Click inside the subtitle box.

4. Type:
   By (Your Name)

If you prefer, you can type:
By John Monyjok Maluth
Or any name you want for practice.

Slide 2: Title and Bullet Points

1. Click Slide 2 thumbnail on the left.

2. Click inside the title box and type:
   Why I Am Learning PowerPoint

3. Click inside the content box (the larger box below).

4. Type these bullet points (press Enter after each line):

- to present my ideas clearly

- to teach or train others

- to use images and charts

- to prepare for school or work

PowerPoint usually creates bullets automatically in the content box. If bullets do not appear, click the Bullets button on the Home tab.

Slide 3: Title and Bullet Points

1. Click Slide 3.

2. Title:
   Where I Will Use PowerPoint

3. Bullets:

- school presentations

- staff meetings

- church teaching and announcements

- training sessions

Now you have a complete mini presentation. It is simple, but it is real.

Step 4: Save Properly (File Name + Folder)

Many beginners lose work because they forget to save early.

Do this now.

A) Save for the First Time

1. Press Ctrl + S (Windows) or Command + S (Mac).

2. If PowerPoint asks where to save, choose:
   Browse (or "This PC") or choose your chosen location

3. Navigate to your folder:
   PowerPoint Practice → My First Presentation

4. File name:
   My First Presentation

5. Click Save.

B) Save Again Often

After saving once, press Ctrl + S regularly.

A good habit:
Save whenever you finish a slide.

C) Use Clear File Names

A good file name answers this:
What is this file, and which version is it?

Examples:

- My First Presentation v1
- My First Presentation v2
- Training Slides February 2026
- Church Youth Seminar Slides

Avoid confusing names like:

- New
- Final
- Final Final
- Final Final Updated

Those names create confusion later.

D) Choose a Safe Folder Location

Choose a folder you can find easily. For many beginners, a safe place is:
Documents → PowerPoint Practice

If you use cloud storage such as OneDrive, it can help with backup, but you should still know where your file is saved.

E) Know Your File Type

Modern PowerPoint saves as:
PPTX

If someone asks you to send the file, you can share the PPTX. If someone asks for a document that opens anywhere, you can export as PDF later, but for now, keep it as PPTX.

5) Quick Checks Before You Close PowerPoint

Before closing PowerPoint, do these checks:

- Are all three slides visible on the left?
- Can you click each slide and see your text?
- Did you save the file in the correct folder?
- Can you find the file using File → Open → Recent?
- Can you open it again after closing PowerPoint?

Beginners become confident when they can close a file and open it again without fear.

That is a real skill.

6) Common Beginner Mistakes (and How to Avoid Them)

Mistake 1: Writing Too Much on One Slide

If your slide is full of text, your audience will read, not listen.

Fix:

- shorten bullets
- use one idea per slide
- speak the details instead of typing everything

Mistake 2: Not Saving Early

People do a lot of work, then the power goes off or the computer hangs.

Fix:

- save as soon as you create the file
- press Ctrl + S often

Mistake 3: Using Hard-to-Read Fonts

Fancy fonts can look nice, but they are hard to read on a projector.

Fix:

- use simple fonts
- use a larger size for titles
- keep good contrast (dark text on light background, or light text on dark background)

Mistake 4: Starting With a Complex Template

Some templates have many shapes and decorations.

Fix:

- start with Blank Presentation while learning
- use simple templates only when you are comfortable

7) A Short Practice Challenge (Optional)

If you have 10 more minutes, improve your mini presentation:

- add a fourth slide titled "What I Want to Improve"
- add three bullets about what you want to learn next (pictures, design, presenting)
- run the slide show using F5 (Windows) or the Slide Show tab

Do not worry if you do not know everything yet. Your job in the beginning is to practice small projects.

Small practice builds strong skill.

What's Next

Next section: PART TWO: THE POWERPOINT WORKSPACE (The Main Window)

In the next part, you will learn the names and purpose of the main areas of PowerPoint, so you can move confidently and find tools without guessing.

PART TWO: THE POWERPOINT WORKSPACE

PowerPoint becomes easy when you understand the workspace. Many beginners struggle not because the tools are difficult, but because they do not know where things are located, what each area is called, and why it exists.

In this part, you will learn:

- the main parts of the PowerPoint window
- how the Ribbon is organized using tabs, groups, and commands
- what the core tabs are for and when to use each one
- file basics you must know so you do not lose work
- how to save, back up, open, and close presentations safely

When you finish, you should be able to open PowerPoint, look at the screen, and say: "I know what this is, and I know where to go next."

1) The Main PowerPoint Window

When PowerPoint opens, you see several areas working together. Each area has a purpose. If you learn these parts early, you will move faster and make fewer mistakes.

A) Title Bar

The Title Bar is the top line of the PowerPoint window. It shows:

- the name of your presentation file
- the program name (PowerPoint)

If your file is not saved yet, PowerPoint may show a temporary name like "Presentation1." That is a warning sign. It means you have work that has not been saved with a proper file name yet.

Good habit:

- Save early so the Title Bar shows your real file name.

B) Quick Access Toolbar

The Quick Access Toolbar is a small set of buttons near the top of the window. It usually contains common commands such as:

- Save
- Undo
- Redo

The reason it exists is simple: it gives you quick access to commands you use often, without switching tabs.

Good habit:

- Keep Save and Undo visible.
- Add any command you use daily.

If you are not sure what a button does, hover your mouse over it. PowerPoint shows a small label describing the command.

C) The Ribbon

The Ribbon is the wide tool strip near the top of PowerPoint. It is the control center.

The Ribbon contains:

- tabs (Home, Insert, Design, and others)
- groups inside each tab (Font, Paragraph, Slides, and so on)
- commands inside each group (buttons and drop-down options)

Your book's main tab set includes Home, Insert, Design, Animations, Slide Show, Review, and View.

Do not fear the Ribbon. Think of it like a toolbox:

- you choose the right tool for the job
- you do not need to memorize everything at once

D) Tabs

Tabs are the top-level categories on the Ribbon. Each tab contains tools for a specific type of work.

Example:

- Home tab is for daily editing (text, slides, formatting)
- Insert tab is for adding objects (pictures, charts, tables, shapes)
- Design tab is for style and themes
- Slide Show tab is for presenting

You will learn what each tab does later in this part.

E) Slide Pane

The Slide Pane is usually on the left side. It shows small thumbnails of your slides. This area helps you:

- move between slides quickly
- see the order of slides
- drag slides to rearrange them
- delete slides you do not want

Many beginners forget this pane exists. They edit one slide and do not notice they are on the wrong slide.

Good habit:

- before typing, glance at the left pane and confirm which slide is selected

F) Workspace

The workspace is the large middle area where you actually build slides. When you click a slide thumbnail on the left, the slide appears in the workspace.

In the workspace, you can:

- type text
- resize text boxes
- insert pictures
- move shapes
- align objects
- design your slide visually

If you only learn one thing today, learn this:

- the slide pane is for navigation
- the workspace is for building

G) Notes Area

Many PowerPoint layouts show a Notes section below the workspace. Notes are for the speaker, not for the audience.

Speaker notes help you:

- remember key points
- avoid writing too much text on the slide
- teach smoothly while keeping slides clean

If you do not see notes, do not worry. You can enable it in the View tab later.

H) Status Bar

The Status Bar is the strip at the bottom of the PowerPoint window. It shows helpful information such as:

- slide number (example: "Slide 2 of 10")
- language tools or proofing status
- view buttons (Normal, Slide Sorter, Reading View in many versions)
- zoom control

Beginners often ignore the Status Bar, but it is a powerful helper.

Good habit:

- use the Zoom slider when you need to see more detail or get a wider view
- use view buttons when you want to reorder slides quickly

These main areas of the PowerPoint window are a foundation for everything else. The file you provided lists the major window components such as the Ribbon, tabs, slide pane, workspace, status bar, title bar, and Quick Access Toolbar.

2) The Key Idea Behind the Ribbon

To use PowerPoint confidently, you must understand how the Ribbon is organized. The Ribbon uses a simple structure:

Tabs → Groups → Commands

A) Tabs

Tabs organize tools by activity.

When you click a tab, the tools you see change. This keeps the screen from being crowded with too many buttons at once.

B) Groups

Inside each tab, the tools are arranged into groups. A group is a small area of related tools.

Example in the Home tab:

- Clipboard group
- Slides group

- Font group
- Paragraph group

Groups help you locate commands quickly.

Tip:

- when you cannot find a tool, ask yourself: "Which tab is it likely to be in?" Then look for a group that matches what you want to do.

C) Commands

Commands are the buttons, menus, and drop-down options you click to do tasks.

Examples:

- New Slide
- Bold
- Align Center
- Insert Picture
- Change Theme
- Start Slide Show

Some commands have small arrows. That usually means:

- there are more options inside the command

Example:

- the New Slide button often has a drop-down arrow that lets you choose a layout

D) Dialog Box Launchers

In many versions, some groups have a tiny arrow in the corner. That arrow opens a dialog box with more settings.

Beginners do not need to master dialog boxes immediately, but you should know they exist.

Simple rule:

- Ribbon shows common options
- dialog box shows extra options

E) Context Tabs and Hidden Tabs

Sometimes you click an object (like a picture, a chart, or a table) and new tabs appear. These are context tabs.

Example:

- click a picture and a Picture Format tab may appear
- click a table and Table Design and Layout tabs may appear

These tabs appear only when relevant, then disappear when you click away.

This is why some people call them "hidden" tabs. Your file includes a chapter called "Other Hidden Tabs," which matches this idea.

Good habit:

- when you click an object and see new tabs, explore them, because those tabs contain the best tools for that object

3) The Core Tabs and What They Are For

Now let's walk through the main tabs one by one. You do not need to memorize everything. You need to understand purpose.

Your goal is to know:

- which tab to use for which task
- what type of tools are inside each tab

A) Home Tab

The Home tab is where you spend most of your time.

Use it for:

- creating and managing slides
- formatting text and paragraphs
- aligning and arranging objects
- basic editing like copy, paste, and find/replace

If you are a beginner, build your first skills here first.

Typical beginner tasks in Home:

- add new slides
- choose slide layouts
- make text bold or change font size
- add bullets and adjust spacing
- align text left or center
- copy formatting using Format Painter

B) Insert Tab

Use the Insert tab to add things to your slide.

Insert is for:

- pictures and screenshots
- shapes and icons
- SmartArt graphics
- charts and tables
- text boxes
- audio and video
- hyperlinks

When your slide looks too empty or too plain, Insert is where you go.

Beginner reminder:

- Insert is powerful, but do not insert too many things on one slide. Keep slides clean.

C) Design Tab

Use the Design tab to control the look and style of your presentation.

Design is for:

- themes
- variants and color sets
- slide size (standard vs widescreen)
- background style

Design helps you make slides consistent. Consistency matters more than decoration.

Beginner rule:

- pick one theme and stick with it
- avoid mixing many fonts and many color styles

D) Animations Tab

Use the Animations tab to control how objects appear, move, or disappear on a slide.

Animations are for:

- making bullet points appear one by one
- highlighting an item when you speak about it
- guiding attention

Animations can help teaching, but they can also distract if overused.

Beginner rule:

- use simple animations
- keep speed moderate
- avoid too many effects on one slide

E) Slide Show Tab

Use Slide Show when you are ready to present.

Slide Show is for:

- starting your presentation from the beginning or current slide
- rehearsing timings
- setting up Presenter View
- configuring show options (loop, kiosk mode, monitors)

Beginner focus:

- learn how to start and exit slide show properly
- learn Presenter View if you present often

F) Review Tab

Review is for checking and collaboration.

Use Review for:

- spelling and proofing
- language settings
- comments and feedback

If you work with others, Review becomes very important.

Beginner habit:

- run spelling check before presenting
- fix obvious mistakes early

G) View Tab

View controls how you see and manage your presentation.

Use View for:

- switching views (Normal, Slide Sorter, Notes Page, Reading View)
- showing rulers, gridlines, and guides
- zoom control options
- opening Slide Master and other views in many versions

View helps you work faster.

Beginner tip:

- Slide Sorter view is excellent for rearranging slides quickly
- Notes Page view helps when you want to print speaker notes

These tabs are the heart of PowerPoint. Once you know which tab does what, you stop guessing and start working.

4) File Basics Beginners Must Know

You can be good at designing slides and still fail if you do not manage files well. Many beginners lose work because they:

- forget where they saved the file
- save with a confusing name
- work directly from a USB drive and lose it
- edit a file attachment without saving a proper copy
- overwrite a good version with a bad version

Let's fix that.

A) Presentation File Types

PowerPoint supports multiple file types. Here are the ones beginners must know.

PPTX

This is the modern PowerPoint file format (PowerPoint 2007 and later).

Use PPTX for:

- normal PowerPoint work
- sharing with people who use modern Office versions
- keeping features like animations and transitions

If someone says "send me the PowerPoint," PPTX is usually what they mean.

PPT

This is the older PowerPoint format (used in PowerPoint 2003 and earlier).

You might use PPT when:

- you are sharing with an older computer
- a specific system or office still uses the old format

But for most people today, PPTX is better.

Important note:

- when you save as PPT, some modern features may not work the same way

PDF Export

PDF is not a PowerPoint editing file. PDF is for sharing and printing.

Export as PDF when:

- you want the slides to look the same on any computer
- you want to send slides to someone who does not need to edit them
- you are submitting a report or handout

PDF is great for stable sharing, but you cannot edit it like a normal PowerPoint file.

PPSX

Some versions allow saving as a PowerPoint Show (PPSX). When someone opens it, it starts directly in slide show mode.

This is useful when:

- you want someone to present without editing
- you are sending a kiosk presentation

Beginners can ignore this for now, but it is good to know it exists.

POTX

A template file format. It is used when you want a reusable design for many presentations.

If you do training programs often, templates can save time.

5) Saving, Save As, and Backups

A) Saving

Save updates your current file.

Good habits:

- save early
- save often

Practical routine:

- press Ctrl + S after completing each slide
- press Ctrl + S before inserting media like video

B) Save As

Save As creates a new copy of your file, usually with a different name or in a different location.

Use Save As when:

- you want a second version
- you want to try changes without risking the original
- you want to create a "final" copy for sharing
- you want to export to another format

A professional versioning habit:

- keep your base file safe
- use Save As to create versions

Example:

- Training Deck v1
- Training Deck v2
- Training Deck v3

This is better than overwriting one file again and again.

C) Backups

Backups protect you from mistakes, power cuts, and computer problems.

Here are safe backup habits for beginners:

1. Use one main folder
   Create a folder for your presentations:

   - Documents → Presentations

Inside it, create subfolders:

- School
- Work
- Church
- Training

2. Keep a backup copy
   Back up your presentation:

   - to an external drive
   - or to cloud storage (OneDrive, Google Drive, or similar)

3. Keep a "clean" copy
   Before making big changes, do:

- File → Save As → add "Backup" in the name

Example:

- Youth Seminar Backup
  Then continue editing your main copy.

4. Understand AutoRecover
   PowerPoint often has AutoRecover, which can restore files after a crash. This is helpful, but do not depend on it.

AutoRecover is not a replacement for saving.

6) Opening and Closing Safely

A) Opening a Presentation

Common safe ways to open a file:

1. From PowerPoint

- File → Open → Recent

- File → Open → Browse

2. From File Explorer

- go to your folder

- double-click the PPTX file

3. Drag and Drop

- drag the PPTX file into PowerPoint

What to avoid:

- editing directly from an email attachment without saving a proper copy

- opening from a random downloads folder and forgetting where the file is

Best practice for attachments:

- download the attachment

- save it in your correct folder

- then open and edit from there

B) Protected View and Read-Only

Sometimes PowerPoint opens a file in Protected View, especially if it comes from the internet or email. This is a safety measure.

If you trust the file source, you can enable editing. If you do not trust it, do not enable editing.

Also, some files open as Read-Only when:

- someone else is using the file

- the file is locked

- you do not have permission to edit it

In that case, use:

- File → Save As → save a copy with a new name
  Then edit your copy.

C) Closing a Presentation Safely

Beginners sometimes click the X and lose work. PowerPoint usually asks you to save, but never rely on that prompt.

Safe closing routine:

1. press Ctrl + S to save
2. confirm your file name and location
3. close the presentation

If you are closing PowerPoint entirely, still do the same routine.

D) Working From USB Drives

USB drives are useful, but they can be risky if:

- you remove the drive while the file is open
- the drive disconnects
- the drive is old and failing

Safer method:

- copy the file from USB to your computer folder
- work on it locally
- save
- then copy the final file back to USB if needed

This protects you from sudden disconnection problems.

7) Practice Tasks for This Part

Do these tasks now to build confidence.

Practice Task 1: Identify the Workspace Parts

Open any presentation and point to these items:

- Title Bar

- Quick Access Toolbar
- Ribbon
- Tabs
- Slide pane thumbnails
- Workspace slide area
- Status Bar
- Zoom control

Say the names aloud if possible. It sounds simple, but it trains your brain fast.

Practice Task 2: Explore Tabs Without Fear

Click each core tab and observe:

- what groups appear
- what tools look familiar
- what tools look new

Do not click randomly. Just observe.

Practice Task 3: Save As a Backup Copy

1. Open your mini project from Part One.
2. Click File → Save As.
3. Save a copy named:
   My First Presentation Backup
4. Close the file.

5. Open both versions and confirm they are separate files.

Practice Task 4: Export to PDF

1. Open your presentation.

2. Export or Save As PDF (depending on your version).

3. Save the PDF in the same folder.

4. Open the PDF and compare it to the PPTX.

This teaches you the difference between an editing file and a sharing file.

8) A Simple Safety Checklist Before You Present

Before you go to a meeting, class, sermon, or training, do this:

- save the file
- make a backup copy
- test it on the presenting computer if possible
- test fonts and layout
- test media (audio/video)
- run the slide show once from beginning to end
- confirm you know where the file is located

This checklist prevents last-minute panic.

What's Next

Next section: PART THREE: BUILDING SLIDES THAT MAKE SENSE

In the next part, we will focus on slide layouts, text, structure, and simple design rules, so your slides communicate clearly without being crowded or confusing.

PART THREE: BUILDING SLIDES THAT MAKE SENSE

PowerPoint is not about decoration. It is about communication.

A presentation can fail even if the colors are beautiful, because the message is unclear. It can also succeed even with a simple design, because the message is clear and easy to follow.

This part teaches you how to build slides that make sense to real people:

- how to choose the right slide layouts
- how to write text that is readable and clean
- how to structure slides so the audience understands quickly
- how to plan a presentation before you start typing
- how to practice by creating a complete 6-slide presentation

If you do the practice project at the end, you will have a full presentation that you can reuse and improve as you learn more tools in later chapters.

1) Slide Layouts: Choose the Right Slide for the Job

A slide layout is the structure of a slide. It controls where titles, text boxes, images, and content placeholders appear.

When you click **Home → New Slide**, PowerPoint creates a slide with a layout. You can change the layout at any time using **Home → Layout**.

Beginners often do one of these two mistakes:

- they use the same layout for every slide
- they force content into a wrong layout and fight the slide

The solution is simple:
Choose the layout that matches your message.

Below are the key layouts you must know.

A) Title Slide

The Title Slide is usually the first slide. It introduces your topic.

It often contains:

- a title
- a subtitle (your name, date, event, organization)

Use a Title Slide when:

- you are starting a presentation
- you want a clear opening
- you want people to know the topic immediately

Best practice for beginners:

- keep the title short and strong
- keep subtitle simple

Example:
Title: Digital Safety for Beginners
Subtitle: Training Session | February 2026 | John Monyjok Maluth

B) Title and Content

This is the most common layout.

It contains:

- a title at the top
- one main content box below

The content box can hold:

- bullet points
- a table
- a chart
- a SmartArt graphic
- a picture

Use Title and Content when:

- you want to explain one main idea
- you want to list points clearly
- you want to combine a title with a simple visual

Beginner tip:
This layout is your daily bread. Learn it well.

C) Two Content

This layout splits content into two side-by-side sections.

It contains:

- a title
- two content boxes below

Use Two Content when:

- you want to compare two things
- you want text on one side and an image on the other
- you want two lists side by side

Examples:

- Pros vs Cons
- Before vs After
- Problem vs Solution
- Steps vs Tools

Beginner warning:
Do not put too much text in both sides. The slide will feel crowded.

D) Section Header

A Section Header slide is like a divider. It announces a new section.

Use Section Header when:

- your presentation has parts

- you want to pause and transition clearly
- you want the audience to reset attention

Example:
Section Title: Part Two: Online Safety
Subtitle: Protect Your Accounts and Devices

This slide is powerful in training and teaching. It helps people follow your flow.

E) When Layout Matters More Than Design

Layout is a communication tool.

If you choose the wrong layout, you create confusion:

- text may look cramped
- visuals may not fit
- the audience may struggle to follow

If you choose the right layout, even a plain design looks professional.

Good habit:
Before typing, ask:
"What layout matches what I am about to say?"

2) Text Basics: Clear Titles, Readable Bullets, Spacing, and Alignment

PowerPoint is a visual medium. People read slides quickly, not slowly.

If your text is unclear, small, or crowded, your audience will stop listening and start struggling.

This section teaches you text rules that work in classrooms, meetings, churches, and trainings.

A) Clear Titles

A slide title should tell the audience what the slide is about.

Bad titles:

- Introduction
- Notes
- Important
- Summary

These titles are too vague.

Better titles:

- Why Digital Safety Matters
- The 3 Most Common Online Scams
- Steps to Create a Strong Password
- What To Do If Your Account Is Hacked

A good title acts like a signboard on a road.

Beginner rule:
Make your title a sentence or a clear phrase that explains the point.

B) Readable Bullets

Bullets are useful, but only when they are short and readable.

Bad bullets:

- long paragraphs copied from a document
- full speeches typed on the slide
- many lines that take the whole screen

Better bullets:

- short phrases
- key words
- simple steps
- few lines

A practical rule for beginners:

- keep 3 to 5 bullets per slide when possible
- keep each bullet short
- speak the explanation, do not type everything

Example of good bullets:

Title: Strong Password Rules
Bullets:

- use at least 12 characters
- mix letters, numbers, symbols
- avoid names and birthdays
- use a password manager if possible

This slide is easy to read and easy to present.

C) Font Size and Readability

A slide might look readable on your laptop, but not on a projector or TV.

Beginner guidelines:

- Titles: 32 to 44 pt (depending on theme)
- Body text: 20 to 28 pt
- Avoid body text smaller than 18 pt if possible

If you must go below 18 pt, it usually means:

- you have too much text
- you need to split the slide into two slides

D) Spacing

Spacing controls how "open" or "crowded" your slide feels.

Common spacing problems:

- lines are too close together
- bullets are packed tightly
- the slide feels heavy

Fixes:

- use line spacing in the Paragraph group
- add space between bullets
- reduce text and give it room

A slide should breathe. When it has space, the audience can read faster.

E) Alignment

Alignment gives order and professionalism.

Common alignment choices:

- Left alignment for most body text
- Center alignment for titles or special slides
- Right alignment rarely used for main content

Beginner rule:

- keep titles consistent (same alignment across slides)
- keep body text consistent

Do not center body bullets unless you have a special design reason. Centered bullets are harder to scan quickly.

F) Consistency

Consistency is one of the easiest ways to look professional.

Consistent means:

- titles look similar across slides
- bullet style is similar across slides
- fonts are similar across slides
- spacing and alignment are similar across slides

Beginners often change style slide by slide. That makes the deck feel messy.

Simple habit:
Pick a style, then repeat it.

3) Good Slide Structure: One Idea per Slide, Less Text, Strong Visuals

Now let's talk about the deeper question: what makes a slide "make sense"?

A slide makes sense when:

- the audience understands it within a few seconds
- the slide supports what you are saying
- the slide focuses on one idea

A) One Idea per Slide

If a slide tries to do two or three different things, the audience gets lost.

Example of a bad slide:
Title: Internet Safety
Bullets:

- passwords
- scams
- viruses
- privacy
- online bullying
- data backups

This is too broad. Each point could be a separate slide.

Fix:
Create multiple slides:

- Password Safety
- Scam Awareness
- Device Protection
- Privacy and Sharing

When each slide has one idea, your presentation becomes easier to teach.

B) Less Text, More Meaning

Slides are not books.

If you want to give full details, you can:

- speak the details while the slide shows keywords
- use speaker notes for yourself
- provide a handout as a PDF later

A good slide gives the audience:

- the structure
- the key message
- the main points

You provide the story.

C) Strong Visuals (Used Wisely)

Visuals can include:

- pictures

- simple icons
- charts
- diagrams
- screenshots (very useful in computer training)

Visuals help when they explain something better than words.

But visuals can also distract when they are:

- random
- too many
- low quality
- unrelated to your message

Beginner visual rule:
Use one strong visual that supports your idea, not five decorations.

Examples of good visuals:

- a screenshot showing where to click
- a simple chart showing growth
- a picture that illustrates a real situation
- an icon set that supports steps (but keep it simple)

D) The Audience Test

Here is a quick test:

If someone looks at your slide for 5 seconds, will they understand what you are talking about?

If the answer is no, simplify:

- shorten title
- reduce bullets
- add a helpful visual
- split into two slides

4) A Simple Presentation Plan (Purpose, Audience, Key Message, Flow)

Many beginners start PowerPoint like this:
Open PowerPoint → start typing → keep adding slides → get stuck → rush at the end.

A better way is to plan first. Planning saves time.

You do not need a long plan. You need a simple plan with four things:

- purpose
- audience
- key message
- flow

A) Purpose

Ask: Why am I presenting?

Common purposes:

- to teach

- to inform
- to persuade
- to train
- to report progress
- to inspire

Your purpose shapes everything:

- the number of slides
- the tone
- the type of visuals
- how much detail you include

B) Audience

Ask: Who is listening?

Audience factors:

- beginners or advanced learners
- students, workers, church members, community groups
- age range and language level
- time available

A training for beginners should use:

- simpler words
- more examples

- more step-by-step screenshots

A report to managers should use:

- fewer slides
- more summary charts
- direct conclusions

C) Key Message

Ask: What is the one main thing I want them to remember?

If the audience forgets everything else, what should remain?

Example key messages:

- "Online safety is a daily habit, not a one-time action."
- "A clean slide helps the audience listen, not struggle."
- "PowerPoint is a tool; your message is the real power."

When you know your key message, you can keep slides focused.

D) Flow

Flow is the order of ideas.

A simple flow pattern:

1. open (title and agenda)
2. explain the main points

3. close with summary and next steps

If you are training, flow can be:

- problem → solution → practice
- steps → demonstration → exercise
- story → lesson → action

Flow keeps your audience from feeling lost.

5) Practice Project: Create a 6-Slide Presentation

Now you will create a complete 6-slide presentation.

You can choose any topic, but to make it easy, I will give you a simple example topic:

Topic example:
"PowerPoint Basics for Beginners"

If you prefer, you can change the topic to something you teach:

- church discipleship lesson
- health and hygiene training
- staff orientation
- academic study skills

The structure remains the same.

Step 1: Create the File and Save It First

1. Open PowerPoint.
2. Choose Blank Presentation.

3. Save immediately:
   File name: PowerPoint Basics for Beginners
   Folder: PowerPoint Practice → Part Three Practice

Saving first protects you from loss.

Step 2: Build the 6 Slides

You will create:

1. Title
2. Agenda
3. Content Slide 1
4. Content Slide 2
5. Content Slide 3
6. Summary

Slide 1: Title Slide

Layout: Title Slide

Title:
PowerPoint Basics for Beginners

Subtitle:
Training Session | Your Name | Date

Tip:
Keep it clean. Do not add extra decorations.

Slide 2: Agenda

Layout: Title and Content

Title:
Agenda

Bullets:

- what PowerPoint is used for
- how the workspace is organized
- how to build simple slides that make sense
- practice: create a 6-slide deck

Agenda slides are helpful in trainings and meetings. They tell people what is coming.

Beginner tip:
Do not list 10 agenda points. Keep agenda short.

Slide 3: Content Slide 1

Layout: Title and Content

Title:
Where PowerPoint Is Used

Bullets:

- school presentations and lessons
- meetings and workplace reporting
- church teaching and announcements
- community training sessions

Optional visual:
Add one small icon or picture that represents "presentation" or "training," but only if it supports the slide. Keep it simple.

Slide 4: Content Slide 2

Layout: Two Content (recommended)

Title:
Clean Slides vs Crowded Slides

Left side (Clean):

- short title
- 3 to 5 bullets
- readable font size
- one helpful visual

Right side (Crowded):

- long paragraphs
- tiny font
- too many bullets
- many decorations

This slide teaches comparison. Two Content is perfect here.

Slide 5: Content Slide 3

Layout: Title and Content

Title:
Three Rules for Beginner Slides

Bullets:

- one main idea per slide
- less text, more speaking

- keep layout and style consistent

Optional:
Add a simple shape or icon beside the rules, but do not overdo it.

Slide 6: Summary

Layout: Title and Content

Title:
Summary

Bullets:

- PowerPoint helps you explain ideas using slides
- the workspace is organized to help you work quickly
- good slides are clear, simple, and focused
- practice makes you confident

Closing line (optional, as a final bullet or a text box):
Next step: Build a real presentation for your next meeting or lesson.

6) Test Your Presentation

Now do a quick test:

1. Press F5 to start from the beginning.
2. Use arrow keys to move forward.
3. Press Esc to exit slide show.

Check these:

- can you read text from a distance?
- are slides clean and not crowded?
- does each slide focus on one idea?
- do titles clearly match the content?

7) Improve It One Step Further

If you want to go beyond beginner level, improve your 6-slide deck in these ways:

- choose one theme in the Design tab
- keep font style consistent
- add one simple visual only where it helps
- keep spacing open and readable
- rehearse a short talk for each slide (one minute each)

This is how real skill grows: small improvements repeated.

What's Next

Next section: PART FOUR: HOME TAB (THE DAILY TOOLS)

In the next part, we will go deep into the Home tab because it contains the tools you will use the most: creating slides, formatting text, working with bullets, copying formatting, and editing faster.

PART FOUR: HOME TAB (THE DAILY TOOLS)

Chapter focus: the tools you will use most often

If you spend enough time in PowerPoint, you will notice a pattern. Most of your work is not "special effects." Most of your work is daily work.

You create slides.
You add text.
You format text.
You arrange objects.
You clean things up.
You fix small mistakes fast.

That is why the **Home tab** matters. In many versions of PowerPoint, it is the first tab you see on the Ribbon, and it holds the common tools you will use again and again. In this chapter, you will learn the Home tab in a practical way, so you can build slides faster and keep them clean.

When you click the **Home** tab, you will usually see these groups: **Clipboard, Slides, Font, Paragraph, Drawing, and Editing.**

Think of these groups as a simple workflow:

- Clipboard: move and reuse content

- Slides: create and manage slides

- Font: make text readable

- Paragraph: shape your text blocks (bullets, spacing, alignment)

- Drawing: add shapes and arrange objects
- Editing: find and fix issues quickly

Before we go group-by-group, let's set a goal for this chapter:

Goal: you should be able to rebuild a small presentation using good layouts, clean text, and consistent formatting, without feeling lost in the menus.

How to open the Home tab and recognize the groups

Here is the simple path:

- Open PowerPoint.
- Look at the Ribbon at the top.
- Click **Home** (often the first tab).
- Notice the group labels under the icons: Clipboard, Slides, Font, Paragraph, Drawing, Editing.

If your screen is small, PowerPoint may hide some buttons behind a tiny arrow or reduce the size of the group. The group names are your clue. When you know the group, you can find the tool.

CLIPBOARD GROUP (cut, copy, paste, and Format Painter)

The **Clipboard group** is about moving content and reusing work. You will use it every time you copy text, paste an image, duplicate shapes, or reuse formatting.

The three basic actions

Cut

- Removes what you selected and keeps it ready to paste somewhere else.

- Use it when something is in the wrong place.

Copy

- Leaves the original where it is and creates a duplicate to paste elsewhere.

- Use it when you want the same style or structure again.

Paste

- Places what you cut or copied into a new location.

These shortcuts are worth memorizing because they save time every day:

- Ctrl + X = Cut

- Ctrl + C = Copy

- Ctrl + V = Paste
  Microsoft lists the same core shortcuts as "frequently used," including Ctrl+M for a new slide and Ctrl+C, Ctrl+V, Ctrl+X for copying and pasting. (Microsoft Support)

Paste options (why pasted text sometimes looks "wrong")

When you paste into PowerPoint, the pasted content can take on the style of the slide you paste into. Sometimes that is good. Sometimes it ruins your slide.

Common paste choices you will see include ideas like:

- Keep the original formatting (good when you want to keep the exact style)

- Match the destination style (good when you want the pasted text to look like the slide)

- Keep text only (good when you copied from a website and you want clean text)

PowerPoint shows paste options because slides can have theme fonts, theme colors, and layout rules. If you paste without thinking, you can end up with mixed fonts and messy spacing.

A simple habit:

- If the pasted text looks strange, undo (Ctrl+Z), then paste again and pick a different paste option.

Format Painter (the fastest way to reuse formatting)

Format Painter helps you copy a look and apply it elsewhere. Microsoft describes it as copying formatting like color, font style, size, or borders. (Microsoft Support)

You will use it when:

- One title looks perfect and you want the next titles to match

- One text box has the right bullet spacing and you want the same spacing elsewhere

- One shape has the right fill and outline and you want other shapes to match

How to use it:

- Select the text or object that already looks right.

- Click **Format Painter**.

- Click or drag over the text or object you want to change.

Important detail:

- If you click Format Painter once, it applies one time.

- If you **double-click** Format Painter, it stays on so you can apply the same formatting to many items. Press Esc to stop. ([Microsoft Support](#))

Keyboard method (very fast):

- Ctrl + Shift + C copies formatting

- Ctrl + Shift + V pastes formatting ([Microsoft Support](#))

Tip for beginners:
If your presentation looks inconsistent, Format Painter can fix it faster than manually changing fonts and colors again and again.

SLIDES GROUP (New Slide, Layouts, Reset, Delete, organizing)

The **Slides group** is where you manage the structure of your presentation: add slides, choose layouts, and keep order.

New Slide (build faster with layout choices)

When you click **New Slide**, PowerPoint gives you layout choices. Layouts are not decoration. Layouts are structure.

A good layout:

- keeps your text aligned
- keeps your slide spacing consistent
- helps your presentation look professional without extra effort

Beginner habit:

- Use layouts instead of drawing text boxes by hand every time.
- If you want a title and bullets, use "Title and Content."
- If you want two sections, use "Two Content."
- If you want a big divider slide, use "Seut:
- Ctrl + M adds a new slide ([Microsoft Support](#))

Layout (choose the right shape for your slide)

Use **Layout** when:

- you pasted content and it broke the slide
- you want to change "Title and Content" to "Two Content"
- you used the wrong layout and want to fix it cleanly

Layout changes are often cleaner than deleting and rebuilding.

Reset (the "clean up my slide" button)

Reset is a beginner's best friend.

Use **Reset** when:

- things moved out of place
- you dragged placeholders and now the slide looks strange
- the spacing feels off and you want to return to the layout's default design

Reset brings placeholders back to how the layout is meant to look.

Delete (remove extra slides safely)

Deleting slides is simple:

- click the slide thumbnail on the left
- press Delete on your keyboard, or use the delete option in the Slides group

Beginner warning:
Before you delete, confirm you are deleting the slide thumbnail, not a text box inside the slide.

Organizing slides (simple habits that prevent chaos)

Even in a small deck, order matters. A clean order makes your message easier to follow.

Good habits:

- Keep your first slide as the title slide.
- Keep your agenda early.
- Group related slides together.
- Put your summary near the end.
- If two slides repeat the same message, merge them.

A quick way to make a copy of a slide:

- Ctrl + Shift + D duplicates the selected slide (Microsoft's shortcut list includes this)

FONT GROUP (clear text rules that make slides readable)

The **Font group** controlsze, bold, italic, underline, and color.

Yes, it looks simple. But text is where most presentations succeed or fail.

The beginner rule: readability beats beauty

A slide is not a book page. Your audience must read it quickly.

Use these rules:

- Use a large title.
- Use fewer words.
- Use a readable font.
- Use strong contrast (dark text on light background, or light text on dark background).
- Avoid tiny text that only you can read on your laptop.

Bold, italic, underline (use with care)

PowerPoint lets you embolden, italicize, underline, and more.

Best practice:

- Use **bold** for emphasis, not for every line.
- Use italics rarely on slides (it can reduce readability from a distance).
- Avoid underline for normal emphasis because people associate it with links.

Keyboard shortcuts (fast and worth knowing):

- Ctrl + B = bold
- Ctrl + I = italic
- Ctrl + U = underl
  Microsoft lists Ctrl+B as a frequently used PowerPoint shortcut.

Font size (simple sizes that usually work)

You do not need perfect numbers, but you do need a consistent range.

Common beginner ranges:

- Titles: 36 to 54
- Body text: 20 to 32
- Notes or footnotes (if you must): 14 to 18 (but try to avoid this on slides)

If you see yourself shrinking text to fit, that is usually a sign your slide has too much content. Split the slide.

Font color (avoid "pretty" that kills reading)

Co fight it.

Good habits:

- Use one main text color.
- Use one accent color for highlights.
- Avoid multiple bright colors in the same paragraph.

If your slide has a background image, make sure text still reads clearly. Add a semi-transparent shape behind text if needed.

Clear text rule: keep it consistent

A presentatioot ten different documents pasted together.

Consistency checklist:

- One or two fonts for the whole deck
- Similar title sizes across slides
- Similar bullet sizes across slides
- Same capitalization style across slides

If one slide looks "different," Format Painter can fix it quickly.

PARAGRAPH GROUP (bullets, alignment, spacing, and structure)

The **Paragraph group** shapes your text blocks: bullets, numbering, alignment, line spacing, indents, and sometimes columns.

This group is where messy slides become clean.

Bullets (make your points easy to scan)

Bullets are not decoration. They are a scanning tool.

Good bullet habits:

- Keep bullets short.
- Keep one idea per bullet.
- Keep the same bullet style across slides.
- Avoid full paragraphs on slides.

A practical limit:

- If you have more than about 6 lines of bullets, consider splitting the slide.

Alignment (your slide looks professional when things line up)

PowerPoint offers alignment choices like left, right, center, and justify.

Beginner default:

- Left align body text.
- Center align titles when it fits the design.

Keyboard shortcuts (fast):

- Ctrl + L = left align
- Ctrl + E = center align
- Ctrl + R = right align
- Ctrl + J = justify

Spacing and indents (where most beginners struggle)

If bullets look crowded, do not change font first. Change spacing first.

Use paragraph tools to:

- increase line spacing a little
- add space after a paragraph
- fix inde simple rule:
- If your slide looks tight, add spacing.
- If your slide looks scattered, reduce spacing and remove extra bullets.

Columns (use only when you truly need them)

Columns can help when you have two short lists that belong together.

But columns can also cause confusion if:

- text wraps awkwardly
- spacing becomes uneven
- the slide becomes too dense

If your content is heavy, use two slides instead of squeezing two columns.

DRAWING GROUP (shapes, quick styles, arranging objects)

The **Drawing group** lets you ly. It is also where you start learning object order and placement.

Shapes are useful for:

- simple diagrams
- arrows and flow
- callouts
- labels
- visual grouping (put a light rect Creating shapes the clean way

When you add a shape:

- keep it simple
- align it with the slide layout
- avoid too many different shape styles on one slide

If you use shapes as "background blocks" behind text:

- use soft colors
- keep outlines thin or remove outlines
- make sure text stays readable

Quick Styles (save time, stay consistent)

Quick Styles exist so you do not manually rebuild the same look each time.

Beginner habit:

- pick one shape style for your deck
- stick with it

Arranging objects (a small skill that changes everything)

Even though "arrange" options show up in different places depending on your version, the ideas stay the same:

- Bring forward / send backward (control what is on top)
- Align (left, center, right, top, middle, bottom)
- Distribute (make spacing even)
- Group (move several items as one)

A simple test:
If movilide, you probably need alignment, distribution, or grouping.

EDITING GROUP (Find, Replace, Select, Selection Pane basics)

The **Editing group** is about cleaning up and controlling your slide objects.

The book file describes Find, Replace, Select, and mentions the **Selection Pane** as a helpful tool when you need to select objects more precisely.

Find (fix repeated issues fast)

Use Find when:

- you spelled a name one way on one slide and differently on another
- you want to check if a word appears too often
- you waa big deck

Replace (change repeated text without hunting slide by slide)

Replace is one of the most practical time savers:

- change a date everywhere
- change a speaker name everywhere
- change "2025" to "2026" everywhere
- fix a repeated spelling error

Beginner warning:
Always check the results after Replace. If your deck has special cases, Replace might change more than you intended.

Select (stop clicking the wrong object)

Select helps when:

- objects overlap
- a shape is behind another shape
- you keep selecting the background instead of the text box

Selection Pane (your control room for messy slides)

When slides get busy, clicking becomes unreliable. The Selection Pane helps you:

- see a list of objects on the slide
- choose the exact object you want
- hide and show objects while editing

If you ever say, open the Selection Pane.

Shortcuts box (Home tab shortcuts you should know)

These shortcuts are not just for experts. They make beginners faster and calmer, because you stop fighting the interface.

Below are shortcuts Microsoft lists as common PowerPoint shortcuts for creating and editing presentations. (

Shortcut	What it does
Ctrl + M	Add a new slide
Ctrl + X	Cut selected text, object, or slide
Ctrl + C	Copy selected text, object, or slide
Ctrl + V	Paste
Ctrl + Z	Undo
Ctrl + Y	Redo
Ctrl + S	Save
Ctrl + B	Bold
Ctrl + I	Italic
Ctrl + U	Underline
Ctrl + Shift + C	Copy formatting
Ctrl + Shift + V	Paste formatting
Ctrl + L	Left align

Shortcut	What it does
Ctrl + E	Center align
Ctrl + R	Right align
Ctrl + J	Justify
Ctrl + Shift + D	Duplicate the selected slide

Extra tip:
Format Painter also supports multi-use when you double-click it, and Microsoft notes you can stop formatting with Esc.

Practice project: rebuild your 6-slide deck using better layout and formatting

You already built a simple 6-slide presentation in Part Three:

- Title
- Agenda
- 3 content slides
- Summary

Now you will rebuild it using the Home tab tools so it looks clean and consistent.

What you will produce

A refreshed 6-slide deck that has:

- consistent layouts

- readable text
- clean bullet structure
- consistent fonts and sizes
- aligned objects
- consistent spacing

Step-by-step workflow (use this every time)

Preparation

- Open your 6-slide file.
- Save a copy with a new name (example: "My Presentation Rebuild").

Slide structure first (Slides group)

- Go slide by slide.
- Choose the best layout for each slide.
- Use Reset if placeholders look messy.
- If a slide has too much text, split it into two slides.

Text cleanup (Font and Paragraph groups)

- Make titles consistent in size and style.
- Make body text consistent in size and style.
- Fix bullet levels so your points are clear.
- Add a little spacing if the slide feels crowded.

Consistency pass (Clipboard group)

- Use Format Painter to match titles across all slides.
- Use Format Painter to match bullet text across all slides.
- If you copied content from outside sources, paste as text only when needed so you avoid mixed formatting.

Visual order and shape cleanup (Drawing group)

- If you used shapes, make them consistent.
- Align shapes with the slide layout.
- Keep colors simple and readable.

Final cleanup (Editing group)

- Use Find to check repeated words, names, dates, and spelling issues.
- Use Replace to fix repeated text fast.
- Use Selection Pane if you struggle to click a specific object.

"What good looks like" checklist

Your deck is in good shape when:

- Every slide has one clear message.
- Titles look like they belong to the same deck.
- Bullets are short and readable.
- You do not see random font changes on one slide.
- You do not see random bullet styles on one slide.

- Objects line up cleanly, not floating slightly off.

Common beginner problems and quick fixes

Problem: one slide looks different from the others

- Fix: use Format Painter on the title and body text.

Problem: pasted text brought strange fonts and spacing

- Fix: undo, then paste using a cleaner paste option, then apply your normal style.

Problem: text is too small

- Fix: reduce the amount of text or split the slide. Do not shrink everything to fit.

Problem: objects keep selecting the wrong thing

- Fix: use Select tools and the Selection Pane.

Quick recap

In this chapter you learned the Home tab as a daily work area:

- Clipboard helps you move content and reuse formatting fast.
- Slides helps you build and organize your deck.
- Font and Paragraph help you make text readable and consistent.
- Drawing helps you add and arrange shapes.
- Editing helps you find, replace, and control objects when slides get busy.

When you can use these six groups well, you can build presentations that look clean without needing advanced tools.

PART FIVE: INSERT TAB (MAKE SLIDES RICH, NOT BUSY)

PowerPoint is not only about typing titles and bullets. The Insert tab is where your slides become more "show" than "tell." In the main window, this tab is designed for adding things like charts, tables, SmartArt, media files, hyperlinks, and headers or footers.

But there is a risk: beginners often use Insert tools to decorate, not to communicate. That is how slides become crowded, confusing, and tiring to read. So the goal of this part is simple:

Use Insert tools to make meaning clearer, not to fill space.

In this section, you will learn what to insert, when to insert it, and how to keep your slides clean while still looking professional.

The core rule: insert with a purpose

Before you insert anything, ask yourself one question:

What job should this object do on the slide?

Here are the most common "jobs" you will insert objects for:

1. To show data clearly (tables and charts)

2. To show a process or relationship (SmartArt, shapes, diagrams)

3. To show a real thing (pictures and screenshots)

4. To help navigation during presenting (hyperlinks and action buttons)

5. To add support material (audio and video)

6. To add slide information (date/time, slide numbers, footer text)

If an object does not do one of those jobs, do not insert it.

When to insert what (table vs chart vs SmartArt vs picture)

Many beginners struggle here because everything looks useful. The trick is choosing the best tool for the message.

Use a TABLE when:

- People must read exact numbers or exact words.
- You have small data that fits in a few rows and columns.
- You want a quick comparison (like "Plan A vs Plan B").

Example: A training schedule table, a price list, a list of tasks per week.

Use a CHART when:

- People need to understand a pattern or change, not exact numbers.
- You want to show growth, decline, ranking, or proportions.

Example: Attendance per month, budget breakdown, progress over time.

Use SMARTART when:

- You are explaining a process, cycle, hierarchy, or relationship.
- You are turning a long bullet list into a visual structure.

Example: Steps of a ministry outreach plan, a workflow for office reporting.

Use a PICTURE when:

- You want people to recognize something instantly.
- You want emotion, realism, or proof.

Example: A photo of a project site, a product image, a ministry event photo.

Use a SCREENSHOT when:

- You are teaching software steps.
- You want to show exactly what people should click or see.

Example: A screenshot of the Ribbon, a dialog box, or a menu.

A simple decision guide (so you do not overthink)

If you only remember one guide from this chapter, remember this:

- Exact details needed → Table
- Trend or comparison at a glance → Chart
- Steps/structure/process → SmartArt

- Real example or proof → Picture
- Teach a computer step → Screenshot

The Insert tab layout (what you will find there)

The Insert tab gives you tools grouped by purpose: Tables, Illustrations, Links, Text, and Media.
Your version may place tools slightly differently, but the purpose stays the same across versions.

Now let's go group by group.

TABLES GROUP (SHOW INFORMATION IN A CLEAR GRID)

The Tables group helps you add tables so you can organize information neatly. This is useful for statistics, lists, and comparisons.

How tables work in PowerPoint

When you insert a table, PowerPoint gives you a grid. You choose how many rows and columns you need, then PowerPoint creates the table.

The book notes that PowerPoint may show a ready grid (example: 10 rows by 8 columns) and you can adjust based on your need.

Two ways to insert a table

1. Quick grid method
   - Insert tab → Table
   - Drag across the grid to select size
   - Click to insert

2. Insert Table dialog method

- Insert tab → Table
- Click "Insert Table" (or similar option)
- Type number of columns and rows
- Click OK

Adding an Excel table

Sometimes the data already exists in Excel. You can copy from Excel and paste into PowerPoint, or insert an Excel sheet object depending on your version. The key point for beginners is this:

If you want the table to look like part of your slide and stay simple, paste it as a normal PowerPoint table.
If you want Excel features inside PowerPoint, embed the Excel object, but that increases complexity.

Table formatting rules for beginners

Tables can destroy a slide if they are too big. Follow these rules:

- Keep tables small. If it does not fit easily, split it across two slides.
- Use bigger text than you think. Many tables look fine on a laptop, then become unreadable on a projector.
- Use light borders. Heavy borders make the slide feel boxed in.
- Use one highlight color only. If everything is highlighted, nothing is highlighted.

- Align numbers properly. For example, align currency values consistently.

Tables create extra tools when selected

When you click inside a table, PowerPoint shows extra tabs for table formatting. The file points out that tables can bring extra tabs such as Design and Format.
This is important: beginners often think they "lost" the table tools. You did not lose them. You just have to click inside the table to see them.

Fast table cleanup checklist

After you insert a table, do these quick cleanups:

- Increase font size until readable.
- Reduce unnecessary grid lines.
- Bold the header row.
- Use one style across the whole presentation.

ILLUSTRATIONS GROUP (PICTURES, SHAPES, SMARTART, CHARTS, SCREENSHOTS)

The Illustrations group is where you insert visual elements such as pictures, clip art, shapes, SmartArt, and charts.

This group can make your slides easier to understand, but it can also create clutter fast. So your rule here is:

One visual is often enough.

Pictures (best practices)

Pictures are powerful because the human mind understands images faster than text. But they must be used with discipline.

Do this:

- Use pictures that support the slide message.
- Crop pictures to remove distractions.
- Keep a consistent style (do not mix random photo styles).
- If the picture is a background, reduce its strength so text is easy to read.

Avoid this:

- Putting five small images on one slide just because you can.
- Using low-quality images that look blurry when projected.
- Using images that have no clear reason.

Shapes (simple diagrams without stress)

Shapes are not only decoration. They are tools for teaching:

- Arrows show direction.
- Boxes show categories.
- Lines show connection.
- Circles show cycles or grouping.

If you can explain something faster with 3 shapes than with 8 bullet points, use shapes.

SmartArt (turn bullets into a clear visual)

SmartArt is best for:

- Steps (Process)
- Levels (Hierarchy)
- Grouping (List)
- Cycles (Cycle)

A common beginner mistake is choosing SmartArt that looks fancy but is hard to read. Choose the simplest SmartArt that does the job.

SmartArt rule:
If your audience must "decode" the graphic, you chose the wrong one.

Charts (show meaning, not decoration)

Charts are used to show patterns. Common chart types and best uses:

- Column chart: compare categories (best beginner choice)
- Line chart: show change over time
- Pie chart: show proportions (use only if there are few parts)
- Bar chart: compare many items with long names

Chart rules:

- Remove unnecessary gridlines if they distract.
- Avoid 3D charts for serious training content.

- Use a clear chart title.

- Use 2–3 colors max.

Screenshots (essential for computer training)

Screenshots are perfect for your type of book because you are teaching PowerPoint itself. A screenshot helps the learner follow exactly what you mean.

Screenshot rules:

- Crop tightly around what you are teaching.

- Add a simple arrow or highlight box if needed.

- Do not screenshot your whole screen if only one small box matters.

LINKS GROUP (HYPERLINKS, ACTIONS, AND INTERNAL NAVIGATION)

The Links group lets you add hyperlinks and actions so you can jump to websites, files, or even specific slides inside your presentation.

This is one of the most useful tools for trainers, teachers, and presenters because it turns a normal slide deck into a navigable tool.

Why links matter in real presentations

Links help you:

- Open a website during training (if internet is available).

- Open a PDF or Word file as supporting material.

- Jump to a "Details" slide when someone asks a question, then return.
- Create a menu slide (like "Choose Topic 1, 2, 3").

Hyperlinks: best practice

When creating a hyperlink, do not link random words like "click here."

Instead:

- Link meaningful text (Example: "Open the registration form").
- Or link an object like a button shape.

Also remember:
Always test your links before presenting.

Internal links for navigation (trainer style)

A very useful method:

1. Create a "Menu" slide with 4 topic buttons
2. Each button links to a topic section slide
3. Add a "Back to Menu" button on each topic slide
4. During training, you can jump around smoothly

This simple method makes your training feel organized and confident.

Action buttons

Action buttons let you set behavior when someone clicks. The file mentions assigning actions for content and controlling what happens on click or hover.

For beginners, keep it simple:

- Use click actions only
- Avoid hover actions unless you are very confident

Link safety tip for presenters

If you are presenting on another computer:

- Put your PowerPoint file and all linked files in one folder.
- Move the whole folder together.

That reduces "missing file" problems.

TEXT GROUP (TEXT BOXES, HEADERS/FOOTERS, DATE/TIME, SLIDE NUMBERS)

The Text group helps you add text-based items such as text boxes, slide numbers, symbols, and date/time.

This group sounds simple, but it can fix many beginner problems.

Text box (when you need it)

You need a text box when:

- Your layout does not have a content placeholder where you want text.
- You want to label a picture or chart.
- You want a callout note on the slide.

Text box rule:
If you add more than 3 text boxes on a slide, pause and check if your layout is wrong.

Headers and footers

Footers help when:

- You want the presentation name at the bottom.
- You want your organization name on every slide.
- You want consistency for training materials.

Beginner warning:
Do not put long sentences in the footer. Footers should be short.

Date, time, and slide numbers

Slide numbers are helpful for:

- Training handouts
- Q&A ("Go to slide 12")
- Reference during teaching

But slide numbers should be small and placed consistently.

MEDIA GROUP (AUDIO AND VIDEO THAT ACTUALLY WORK)

The Media group allows you to insert video and audio to improve learning and attention.

The file explains that you can add films and sound to increase the value of your slide show.
It also notes you can insert existing audio files and use clip organizers depending on your setup.

When media is a good idea

Media is useful when:

- You are teaching pronunciation, music, or language.
- You are showing a short real-life example.
- You want a quick testimony or field clip in ministry training.
- You are demonstrating a process that is hard to describe with text.

When media is a bad idea

Avoid media when:

- The clip is too long.
- The clip is not essential to your message.
- The presentation must run on many unknown computers and you cannot control file compatibility.

Beginner media rules (to avoid embarrassment)

1. Keep videos short. If it is more than 60–90 seconds, consider trimming.
2. Test playback on the exact computer you will present from.
3. Keep media files in the same folder as the PowerPoint file.
4. Use "Start on click" unless you truly need autoplay.
5. Lower the volume in advance and test speakers.

Common playback problems and simple fixes

Problem: Video does not play on another computer
Fix: The video may be linked, not embedded. Keep files together, or embed properly.

Problem: Audio is too loud
Fix: Use playback settings or reduce file volume before inserting.

Problem: Video plays but no sound
Fix: Check Windows volume, speaker output selection, and file codec support.

PRACTICE PROJECT: Build one "Training Deck" slide that is rich, not busy

Your task is to create ONE slide that contains:

- One table
- One image
- One chart
- One hyperlink

This practice will train your judgment: the real skill is not inserting items. The real skill is choosing and arranging them so the slide remains readable.

Step A: Create the slide base

1. Create a new blank presentation (or open your practice deck).
2. Add a new slide using a simple "Title and Content" layout.

3. Title the slide: "Training Snapshot"

Step B: Insert the table (small and readable)

1. Insert tab → Table
2. Choose 3 columns × 4 rows
3. Fill it with sample training data like:

- Topic | Time | Trainer
- PowerPoint Basics | 30 min | John
- Insert Tab | 30 min | John
- Practice | 20 min | John

Formatting rules:

- Bold the top row.
- Keep borders light.
- Make sure the font is readable.

Step C: Insert one image (support the message)

1. Insert tab → Pictures
2. Choose a simple image related to training (classroom, laptop, projector, or a clean icon-style photo)
3. Resize it so it does not fight the table for attention.

Rule:
If the image forces you to shrink the table text too much, the image is too big.

Step D: Insert a chart (simple, not fancy)

1. Insert tab → Chart
2. Choose a Column chart
3. Enter sample data like:

- Attendance Week 1: 15
- Attendance Week 2: 22
- Attendance Week 3: 18

Chart rules:

- Remove extra clutter (too many labels, too many colors).
- Use a clear chart title like "Attendance Trend"

Step E: Add one hyperlink (trainer-friendly)

You have two good options:

Option 1: Link text

- Insert tab → Link
- Type text on the slide: "Open course resources"
- Link it to a website (only if internet will be available)

Option 2: Link to another slide

- Create a second slide titled "Resources"
- Add a few bullet items
- Go back to your "Training Snapshot" slide

- Link "Open course resources" to the "Resources" slide

Step F: Clean up the slide so it stays readable

Use this final checklist:

- Can you understand the slide in 5 seconds?
- Is the title clear and specific?
- Are the table words readable from far?
- Is the chart easy to understand without explanation?
- Does the image support the message instead of distracting?
- Does the link look clickable and meaningful?

If any answer is "no," remove something or resize it.

Key habits to carry into the next parts

- Insert tools are not decorations. They are message tools.
- If you insert many objects, your slide will usually lose clarity.
- A clean slide with one strong table or one strong visual often beats a crowded slide with everything.

PART SIX: DESIGN TAB (MAKE IT LOOK CLEAN AND CONSISTENT)

The Design tab is where your presentation stops looking like "six separate slides" and starts looking like "one complete deck." It helps you apply one look across every slide, so your audience pays attention to your message instead of noticing mismatched colors, random fonts, and different backgrounds.

In the PowerPoint guide you shared, the Design tab is presented as a place to control three big areas: Page Setup (slide size and orientation), Themes (a unified style), and Background (how the slide surface looks).

This part will teach you beginner-friendly rules for clean design, then show you how to use the Page Setup, Themes, and Background groups, and finally walk you through a practice project to redesign your 6-slide deck using one theme and readable backgrounds.

1) Design rules for beginners

You do not need to be an artist to make clean slides. You need a few rules, and you need to follow them every time.

A) Contrast (make text easy to read fast)

Contrast is the difference between two things, especially text and background. If your audience struggles to read your slide, your message dies before it starts.

Simple contrast rules you can follow every time:

- Use dark text on light backgrounds, or light text on dark backgrounds. Avoid "medium on medium."

- Use big font sizes. If you must squint, it is too small.

- Do not place text directly on busy photos unless you add a solid overlay behind the text.

- Avoid light colors for body text (yellow, light green, light blue) unless the background is very dark.

- Limit the number of colors used for text. Most slides can work with:

    o one main text color (often black or very dark gray)

    o one accent color for headings or key words

A quick test:
Stand back from your screen. If you cannot read the slide title and the first line of content, increase contrast by changing color, making text bigger, or simplifying the background.

B) Alignment (make everything look intentional)

Alignment is the difference between "I placed things anywhere" and "I designed this."

When objects line up, the slide looks calm and professional. When objects do not line up, the slide looks noisy even if the content is good.

Alignment habits that instantly improve slides:

- Pick one invisible left edge, and align most text and objects to it.

- Use PowerPoint's Align tools (Align Left, Align Center, Align Right) for shapes, text boxes, and pictures.

- Use "Distribute" to space objects evenly when you have multiple boxes or images.

- Keep headings aligned the same way on every slide (usually left-aligned for training decks).

Beginner trick:
Turn on Guides and Gridlines (usually found under View). Then align text boxes and images to those lines. You will feel like you suddenly became "good at design."

C) Spacing (give content room to breathe)

Crowded slides make people tired. Clean slides feel easier.

Spacing is not "empty space." It is breathing room that makes your content readable.

Spacing rules you can use on every slide:

- Keep the same margins on each slide (top, left, right, bottom).

- Do not push text to the edges of the slide.

- Add space between title and content.

- Add space between paragraphs or bullet groups.

- Use consistent line spacing. If one slide has tight lines and another has wide lines, the deck feels messy.

A simple spacing method:
Pick a "standard padding" for your deck (example: keep at

least one finger-width of space between the edge of the slide and any content). Do it on every slide.

D) Consistency (repeat what works)

Consistency is the secret of "professional." The audience may not explain it, but they feel it.

What should stay consistent across your deck:

- The same theme (colors + fonts)
- The same title style (size, color, placement)
- The same body text style
- The same background style
- The same image style (similar borders, similar shapes, similar tone)
- The same icon style (do not mix different icon sets)

When you keep these consistent, your deck feels like one message, not six unrelated pages.

2) Page Setup group (slide size, orientation, standard vs widescreen)

Before you touch themes and backgrounds, set your slide size. Slide size affects how everything fits: photos, text boxes, charts, and spacing.

The guide you shared highlights Page Setup as part of the Design tab's role in controlling the slide layout.

A) Slide size: Standard (4:3) vs Widescreen (16:9)

PowerPoint commonly offers two main sizes:

Standard (4:3)

- More square.
- Often used with older projectors or older slide libraries.
- Sometimes preferred for printed handouts because it can feel more compact.

Widescreen (16:9)

- Wider and modern.
- Best for modern screens, TVs, and most projectors today.
- Gives more horizontal space, which often helps with clean layouts.

Which one should you choose?

- If you will present on modern screens: choose Widescreen (16:9).
- If you know the projector is old or you must match a school's older template: choose Standard (4:3).
- If you are unsure: Widescreen is usually the safer choice today.

B) Orientation: Landscape vs Portrait

Most slide shows are Landscape (wide). Portrait is rare for live presentations but can be useful for:

- posters
- infographic-style slides

- documents designed to be read vertically on phones

For beginner decks and classroom presentations, keep Landscape unless you have a strong reason not to.

C) Set slide size early (avoid rework)

Changing slide size after designing can cause:

- cropped images
- shifted text boxes
- strange spacing
- layouts that no longer look balanced

If you must change it later, PowerPoint often offers choices like "Maximize" or "Ensure Fit."

- "Ensure Fit" is safer for text-heavy slides because it tries to keep content visible.
- "Maximize" may crop images and push objects off the slide.

Beginner rule:
Set slide size before you design your first real slide.

3) Themes group (choosing a theme, variants, keeping consistency)

A theme is a built-in set of:

- colors
- fonts
- effects (like shape styles)

When you apply a theme, PowerPoint tries to make every slide look like it belongs together. The guide you shared describes the Themes group as a place to pick a ready-made look that unifies the presentation.

A) Choosing a theme (how beginners should decide)

Do not choose a theme because it looks "fancy." Choose one that supports readability.

Pick a theme that is:

- clean and simple
- not overloaded with background graphics
- readable for titles and body text
- appropriate for your audience (students, business, church, training)

Avoid themes that:

- have heavy patterns behind text
- use decorative fonts that slow reading
- rely on weak contrast (gray text on gray background)
- add shapes everywhere (visual noise)

Beginner rule:
If your theme needs a lot of fixing to become readable, it is not the right theme.

B) Variants (small changes without breaking the deck)

Most themes offer Variants. Variants usually change the color arrangement while keeping the same overall style.

Use variants when:

- you like the theme style, but want different colors
- you need a darker version for photo backgrounds
- you want your accent color to match a logo or brand

Beginner rule:
Pick one variant and stay with it across the whole deck. Mixing variants across slides can make your deck feel inconsistent.

C) Keep consistency (how themes help you stay disciplined)

Themes make it easier to stay consistent, but only if you stop fighting them.

How beginners accidentally break a theme:

- using too many manual font changes
- copying a slide from another deck with a different theme
- applying random colors to headings
- changing background styles per slide without a plan

How to protect consistency:

- Use the theme fonts. Do not mix five fonts.
- Use the theme colors. Do not create new colors on every slide.

- If you copy a slide from another deck, use "Keep Destination Theme" when pasting, so it matches your deck.

D) A clean theme formula you can follow

If you want a simple "professional look" without stress, use this formula:

- Heading font: bold, clean, large
- Body font: simple, readable
- Main text color: very dark (or white on dark slides)
- Accent color: one strong color (used for headings, icons, highlights)
- Background: simple, low-noise

This formula works for training decks, classrooms, workshops, and meetings.

4) Background group (background styles, images, keeping readability)

Background is not decoration. Background is a stage. If the stage is too loud, the speaker becomes weak.

The guide you shared describes the Background group as the place to change background styles, use images, and manage background graphics.

A) Background styles (what beginners should use)

Common background options include:

- solid color
- gradient

- picture/texture
- pattern fill

Best backgrounds for beginners:
- solid light gray or white with dark text
- solid dark color with white text
- very subtle gradient (almost invisible)
- a blurred, darkened photo with an overlay

Backgrounds beginners should avoid:
- busy textures behind text
- high-contrast patterns
- bright photos with no overlay

B) Using background images without ruining readability

Photos can look powerful, but they can also kill readability.

If you want to use photos as backgrounds, use these rules:

Rule 1: Put text on a "quiet" area
Choose images with empty space where text can sit (sky, wall, floor).

Rule 2: Use an overlay
Add a semi-transparent rectangle (dark or light) behind your text.

- If the photo is bright, use a dark overlay behind text.

- If the photo is dark, use a light overlay behind text.

Rule 3: Do not use many background photos
For a beginner deck, one background style across slides is cleaner. If you use photos, use one consistent photo style:

- same tone (all dark or all light)
- similar subject type (all office scenes, all nature scenes, etc.)
- similar blur/overlay approach

Rule 4: Keep the title readable first
If the title is not readable in one second, the slide is failing.

C) Apply background to all slides, or use it intentionally

A common beginner mistake is changing the background on every slide. That creates a scattered look.

Better options:

- Use one background for the whole deck.
- Or use two background styles with a clear purpose, for example:
    - Style A for content slides
    - Style B for section breaks or title slides

If you do this, keep it predictable.

5) Practice project: Redesign your 6-slide deck with one theme and readable backgrounds

Now you will apply everything you learned. The goal is not "pretty." The goal is "clean and consistent."

The project goal

Redesign your existing 6-slide deck so that:

- It uses one slide size (Standard or Widescreen).
- It uses one theme (and one variant).
- It uses one background style (or two styles with a clear purpose).
- Every slide has readable text.
- Titles and content align the same way across slides.
- Spacing feels balanced and consistent.

Step 1: Set your slide size first

1. Go to the Design tab.
2. Find the Slide Size option (or Page Setup in older versions).
3. Choose Widescreen (16:9) unless you need Standard (4:3).
4. Confirm your choice and check that nothing is cut off.

Step 2: Pick one theme and commit to it

1. In the Design tab, open the Themes gallery.
2. Choose a simple theme that looks calm and readable.
3. Select one variant you like.
4. Apply it to all slides.

Discipline rule for this project:
Do not change fonts manually unless you have a strong reason.

Step 3: Choose one background style that supports reading

Option A (easiest and cleanest):

- Light solid background + dark text

Option B (strong and modern):

- Dark solid background + white text

Option C (photo background, but controlled):

- One photo style used across slides, with consistent overlay behind text

Apply your choice to the whole deck.

Step 4: Fix titles first (make the deck feel unified fast)

Go slide by slide and make sure:

- Every title is in the same position
- Every title uses the same font, size, and color
- Every title is aligned the same way (usually left)

If you do only this, the deck will already look more professional.

Step 5: Clean up alignment and spacing on every slide

For each slide:

- Align text boxes to the same left edge.

- Keep the same top margin for titles.
- Keep similar spacing between title and content.
- Use consistent bullet spacing if you use bullets.
- Keep consistent image placement if a slide has an image.

A simple method to keep spacing consistent:
Use one "content box width" for all content slides. Copy it from one slide and paste it to others, then replace the content.

Step 6: Redesign your 6 slides using a clear pattern

Here is a simple pattern you can apply:

Slide 1: Title slide

- Big title
- Small subtitle or your name
- Clean background
- Minimal extra text

Slide 2: Agenda or outline

- Title: "What we will cover"
- 3–5 short bullets
- No long sentences

Slide 3: Main point slide

- One key idea

- 3 supporting bullets max
- Highlight one keyword using the theme accent color

Slide 4: Visual slide

- One image that supports the topic
- Short caption or one sentence
- Keep image style consistent (same border or no border throughout)

Slide 5: Example or mini-demo

- Use a two-column layout:
    - left: steps or points
    - right: screenshot or simple diagram

Slide 6: Closing slide

- Summary (2–3 bullets)
- Next step or call to action
- Thank you

If your content is different, keep the design pattern anyway.

Step 7: Do a readability check (the "10-second test")

Open Slide Show view and test each slide:

- Can you read the title instantly?
- Can you read the main content without effort?

- Is there any slide where the background fights the text?
- Do the slides feel like one deck?

If a slide fails, fix contrast first, then spacing, then alignment.

Step 8: Final consistency checklist

Before you finish, verify:

- The same theme is applied to every slide.
- The same fonts are used across slides.
- Titles sit in the same location.
- Colors are limited and repeat with purpose.
- Background style is consistent.
- Images look like they belong together.
- Nothing is too close to the slide edge.

When you can say "yes" to these, your deck will look clean.

Key takeaway

A clean deck is built by rules, not by luck.

If you control contrast, alignment, spacing, and consistency, then the Design tab becomes your tool for discipline: correct size, one theme, and backgrounds that support reading. The result is a presentation that looks unified, calm, and professional, even if you are a beginner.

PART SEVEN: ANIMATIONS AND TRANSITIONS (USE WITH CONTROL)

Animations and transitions are like seasoning. A little can make your message clearer and your delivery smoother. Too much can ruin the whole meal.

This part teaches you how to use motion with control, especially for beginner-friendly presentations, training decks, school work, ministry teaching, and workplace reporting. You will learn how to preview effects before presenting, how to animate objects in the right order with clean timing, how to apply slide transitions without distraction, and how to practice by animating only two slides in your deck.

The goal is not to impress people with effects. The goal is to guide attention, support understanding, and keep the audience listening instead of fighting your slides.

The rule: animation supports the message, not the ego

Here is the mindset that makes animations useful:

- If an effect helps people understand what you are saying, it belongs.

- If an effect exists only to show off, it should go.

Why this rule matters:

- Your audience is not watching a movie. They are trying to follow ideas.

- Motion pulls attention. When everything moves, the audience does not know where to focus.

- Too many effects can make you look less professional, not more.

Think of animation as a pointer. It should point to the next idea, not distract from the idea.

A quick map: Animations vs Transitions

Beginners often mix these up, so let's make it clear.

Animations:

- apply to objects on a slide (text, bullets, pictures, shapes, charts)
- control how items appear, move, or disappear on the same slide

Transitions:

- apply to the slide itself
- control how one slide changes to the next

If you remember only one sentence:
Animations are inside the slide. Transitions are between slides.

When animations and transitions are worth using

Use animation when you want to:

- reveal bullet points one by one as you explain them
- bring attention to one part of a diagram
- show steps in a process, one step at a time
- avoid dumping too much information on the screen at once

Use transitions when you want to:

- create smooth movement from slide to slide
- avoid hard, sudden changes that feel abrupt
- keep a consistent rhythm in the slide show

For a beginner deck, that is often enough.

The most common beginner mistakes (and how to avoid them)

Mistake 1: Animating everything

If every title, every bullet, every icon, and every picture flies in, your deck becomes tiring.

Fix:

- Animate only what you are actively explaining.
- Leave titles static most of the time.
- Use one entrance effect for the whole deck if you are animating bullets.

Mistake 2: Using many different effects

Slide 1: Fly In
Slide 2: Bounce
Slide 3: Wheel
Slide 4: Swivel
This feels random.

Fix:

- Pick one simple effect (Fade or Wipe).
- Repeat it.

Mistake 3: Effects that are too fast or too slow

Too fast feels chaotic. Too slow feels childish.

Fix:

- Keep durations moderate.
- Practice the pacing while speaking.

Mistake 4: Sounds on transitions

Transition sounds often make a deck feel like a game show.

Fix:

- Avoid sounds in most professional, school, and training decks.
- If you use sound, use it for a very specific reason.

Mistake 5: Not previewing

Many problems only appear when you preview or run the slide show.

Fix:

- Preview each animated slide.
- Run the slide show once from start to finish before presenting.

PREVIEW GROUP (check before presenting)

The Preview group exists for one job: to let you see what your audience will see before you show it live.

Your file explains that the Preview group gives a "sneak peek" of how slides will be perceived, including text and chosen animations. It also notes a key beginner detail: the Preview group does nothing until you have selected a slide and added text plus an animation.

That detail matters because beginners often click Preview and think PowerPoint is broken.

How to use Preview properly

1. Click the slide thumbnail you want to test.
2. Click the object on the slide (text box, picture, shape) that has the animation.
3. Confirm an animation is applied.
4. Click Preview.
5. Watch the effect and judge it with these questions:
    - Is it readable?
    - Is it smooth?
    - Is it too fast?
    - Does it match what I want to say?

A simple preview habit

Preview is not something you do once at the end. Use it like spellcheck.

- Apply effect
- Preview
- Adjust
- Preview again

If you do this, you will avoid most embarrassing animation mistakes.

ANIMATIONS GROUP (object animations, order, timing)

The Animations group is where you choose and manage effects for objects. Your file describes this group as offering multiple styles such as fade, wipe, and fly-in. It also mentions the idea of getting more options by clicking the arrow near an effect, and it points to a "Custom Animation" button for deeper control.

Let's translate that into practical beginner use.

Step 1: Choose the right type of animation

Most PowerPoint versions group animations into types like:

- Entrance (how an object appears)

- Emphasis (how an object is highlighted while on the slide)

- Exit (how an object leaves)

- Motion Paths (how an object moves along a path)

For beginners, your safest path is:

- Use Entrance for bullet points and simple reveals

- Use Emphasis only when you have a clear reason

- Avoid Exit and Motion Paths unless you are confident

Why avoid Exit and Motion Paths early:

- They are easy to misuse

- They can confuse the audience
- They can break your pacing if done without planning

Step 2: Pick a "default" effect and stick to it

Here are two effects that work in almost every setting:

- Fade (clean and calm)
- Wipe (useful for step-by-step reveals)

Your file mentions fade and wipe as examples of available styles.

Beginner rule:
Pick one effect for your deck, then repeat it. Consistency makes you look professional.

Suggested default:

- Fade for most training decks

Step 3: Understand order (what happens first, second, third)

Order is the sequence in which animations play.

A clean training slide might look like this:

1. Title appears (usually no animation)
2. Bullet 1 appears
3. Bullet 2 appears
4. Bullet 3 appears
5. A picture appears

6. A key phrase is emphasized

If the order is wrong, your slide can reveal the wrong point at the wrong time.

The most common order problems

- Bullet 3 appears before Bullet 1
- A picture appears too early and distracts from the explanation
- Multiple items appear together when you wanted them one by one

How to control order

In most PowerPoint versions, you can manage order using an animation list (often shown as the "Animation Pane" or a similar panel). If your version does not show a pane by default, look for a button in the Animations tab that opens the list.

Once the list is open, you can:

- drag items up or down to reorder
- select an animation and change its start timing
- adjust duration and delay

Beginner tip:
If a slide has more than 6 animation steps, pause and simplify. Too many steps increases the chance of mistakes during presenting.

Step 4: Understand timing (start, duration, delay)

Timing is what makes animations feel professional.

You usually control timing using three main settings:

Start:

- On Click (you control it)
- With Previous (plays at the same time as the previous animation)
- After Previous (plays automatically after the previous animation finishes)

Duration:

- how long the animation takes to complete

Delay:

- how long PowerPoint waits before starting the animation

The best beginner start setting

For bullet teaching slides:

- Use "On Click" so you control the pace while speaking.

For grouped visuals (example: an icon and a caption that should appear together):

- Use "With Previous" so they appear at the same time.

For automatic sequences (use carefully):

- Use "After Previous" only when you are sure it will match your speaking pace.

Timing rules that keep things clean

- Keep durations consistent across slides.
- Avoid extremely slow effects unless you are doing a dramatic reveal for one key moment.
- If an animation feels like it interrupts your speaking rhythm, reduce the duration.

A practical target range many presenters like:

- 0.3 to 0.8 seconds for simple entrances
  This is not a law, just a good starting range.

Step 5: Basic "custom animation thinking" (plan before you apply)

Your file mentions using "Custom Animation" for greater control. The real lesson here is not the button. The real lesson is the thinking.

Before you animate, ask these four questions:

1. What is the single message of this slide?
2. What should the audience see first?
3. What must wait until I explain it?
4. What should never move at all?

If you answer those questions, your animations become simple and effective.

A clean pattern for training slides (works almost every time)

- Keep the title static
- Animate bullets one by one

- Show the visual after the bullets (or alongside the bullet that mentions it)

- Use one emphasis effect only, if needed, to highlight the key takeaway

If you follow this pattern, your slides will feel controlled and your delivery will feel confident.

TRANSITIONS GROUP (slide transitions, speed, sounds, when to avoid)

Transitions control how slides change from one to the next. Your file describes the Transition group as offering many transitions and the ability to refine them using sound and speed (tempo). It also explains that you can control whether transitions happen automatically after a set time or require a click.

Let's turn that into a beginner-friendly approach.

Step 1: Choose one transition (or none)

For most beginner decks, one transition is enough.

Best simple transitions:

- Fade

- Wipe (used carefully)

If you are presenting serious content (training, reporting, academic work), you can also choose:

- no transition effect (the default simple change) This is still professional.

Beginner rule:
Do not mix multiple transitions across slides unless you have a specific reason, like separating sections.

Step 2: Set a reasonable speed

Transition speed should feel smooth, not dramatic.

- Too fast feels harsh.
- Too slow feels like the slide is dragging.

Start with a moderate duration. Then test in slide show mode.

Step 3: Avoid transition sounds in most decks

Your file notes that you can pick a transition sound.

In most professional and training settings, sounds are a distraction.

Use sounds only when:

- you are building a fun children's presentation
- you are doing a special event with a playful tone
- you are certain the sound system is working and the sound adds value

Otherwise:

- keep sounds off

Step 4: Click vs automatic transitions

Your file highlights the choice between automatic transitions after a set time and transitions that require a click.

For beginners, click-based transitions are safest because they match real speaking.

Use click transitions when:

- you are speaking live
- you want full control
- you are teaching and responding to audience reactions

Use automatic transitions only when:

- you are exporting a self-running presentation
- you are creating a kiosk display
- you have rehearsed timing carefully

Beginner warning:
Automatic transitions can create panic if you are not ready for the next slide yet.

When to avoid animations and transitions altogether

There are times when the cleanest deck is the best deck.

Avoid heavy animation when:

- your audience is reading complex information
- you are presenting in a setting with laggy equipment
- you are short on time and cannot test
- your slides already have enough content movement (videos, live demos)

Avoid transitions when:

- the deck is very technical and people need quick slide changes
- you are jumping around using hyperlinks and slide navigation
- you are in a fast Q&A session

A calm deck can still be powerful.

Practice project: Animate only 2 slides in your deck with simple effects and proper timing

Now you will do the most important thing: practice with discipline.

Your project rules:

- You will animate only two slides.
- You will use one simple animation effect.
- You will keep timing controlled.
- You will use one simple slide transition across the whole deck.
- You will preview and test in slide show mode.

This will train your judgment. Once you can do "simple and clean," you can handle more complex work later.

Step A: Prepare your deck safely

1. Open your 6-slide deck.
2. Save a copy:
    - File name example: "6-Slide Deck (Animated Version)"

3. Make sure your slide order is correct:
    - Title
    - Agenda
    - Content 1
    - Content 2
    - Content 3
    - Summary

Step B: Add one clean transition to all slides

1. Click the first slide thumbnail.
2. Go to the Transitions area (in some versions it is part of the Animz/Transitions tools; your file calls it the Transition group).
3. Choose a simple transition:
    - Fade is a safe choice.
4. Set the transition duration to a moderate speed.
5. Confirm sound is OFF.
6. Click "Apply to All" (or the equivalent button) so every slide changes the same way.

Test quickly:

- Run the slide show and move from slide to slide.
- The transitions should feel smooth and quiet.

Step C: Choose the two slides to animate

Pick two content slides, not the title slide.

Recommended choices:

- Slide 3 (Content Slide 1): bullet teaching slide
- Slide 5 (Content Slide 3): rules slide or steps slide

Why these work well:

- They have clear bullet points
- They benefit from "reveal as you speak"

Step D: Animate Slide 3 (bullets one by one)

Goal:

- Bullets appear one at a time as you click, so the audience focuses on the point you are explaining.

Steps:

1. Go to Slide 3.
2. Click inside the content box that contains your bullets.
3. Apply an entrance animation:
    - Use a simple effect such as Fade (your file lists fade among the available styles).
4. Set Start to:
    - On Click
5. Make sure bullets animate one by one (not all at once).

> - In many versions, this is controlled by "Effect Options" or a similar setting for text animation.

6. Set duration to a moderate speed.

7. Preview the slide using the Preview group. Your file explains preview shows your slide with the chosen animations and is meant to help you catch mistakes before presenting.

Your test:

- Do the bullets appear in the right order?
- Does the pace match your speaking?
- Is anything distracting?

Fix if needed:

- If bullets appear too fast, increase duration slightly.
- If bullets all appear together, change the text animation to "by paragraph" (wording varies by version).

Step E: Animate Slide 5 (one simple reveal plus one emphasis)

Goal:

- Reveal the bullets one by one
- Add a gentle emphasis on the final key takeaway (optional)

Steps:

1. Go to Slide 5.

2. Click the bullet list.
3. Apply the same entrance effect you used on Slide 3.
    - Same effect, same style, same deck rhythm.
4. Set Start to:
    - On Click
5. Preview.

Optional emphasis (only if it supports the message):

1. Click the key takeaway line or a key phrase.
2. Add a gentle emphasis animation (not a wild effect).
3. Set it to start:
    - After Previous (so it happens after the last bullet appears), or On Click (if you want control)

If the emphasis feels like a distraction, remove it. Simple wins.

Step F: Preview both slides carefully

Use Preview on each animated slide. The file warns that previewing depends on having a slide selected and an animation applied.

Preview checklist:

- Does the motion guide attention?
- Does anything feel childish?
- Does anything cover other content?

- Does the timing match how you will speak?

Step G: Full slide show test (the final proof)

1. Start the slide show from Slide 1.
2. Click through normally.
3. Pay attention to your animated slides:
    - Are you clicking too much?
    - Are you losing your place?
    - Do you feel in control?

If you feel out of control, reduce complexity:

- remove emphasis
- reduce the number of animated items
- keep only bullet-by-bullet entrances

This is how you build skill safely.

Troubleshooting (quick fixes for common problems)

Problem 1: Preview does nothing

Likely cause:

- no animation is applied, or the wrong object is selected

Fix:

- select the slide
- select the object

- confirm an animation exists
- then preview (as the file notes, preview depends on these prerequisites).

Problem 2: Bullets appear all at once

Fix:

- adjust text animation options so it reveals "by paragraph" (wording varies)

Problem 3: The animation order is wrong

Fix:

- open the animation list/pane and reorder items

Problem 4: The slide feels too busy

Fix:

- remove half the animations
- keep only the bullet reveal

Problem 5: Transitions feel annoying

Fix:

- reduce duration
- remove sounds (recommended for most decks)
- consider using no transition effect at all

A simple "control checklist" before you present

Before you present any deck that uses motion, do this:

- Preview the animated slides.

- Run the slide show once start to finish.
- Confirm transitions are consistent.
- Confirm sounds are off unless you truly need them.
- Confirm click timing feels natural.
- Confirm you can present without thinking about the effects.

If you can present smoothly without worrying about the effects, you used animations the right way.

What's next

Next section: PART EIGHT: SLIDE SHOW TAB (PRESENT LIKE A PRO)

PART EIGHT: SLIDE SHOW TAB (PRESENT LIKE A PRO)

When people say "PowerPoint is easy," they usually mean building slides. Presenting is a different skill. The Slide Show tab is where you turn a set of slides into a real talk: paced, readable, smooth, and controlled.

This part will teach you how to start your show the right way, rehearse and time yourself, record narrations when it truly adds value, set up show options (including hiding slides and looping), use Presenter View on one or two screens, and rely on key shortcuts so you stay in control even when something goes wrong.

(These core tools are the same ones introduced under the Slide Show tab: starting options, rehearsal tools, show setup options, monitors, Presenter View, and key shortcuts like F5 and Shift+F5.)

1) Starting Slide Show: from beginning, from current, custom show

In real life, you do not always present from Slide 1. Sometimes you are asked to "jump to the main point," or you want a shorter version for a different audience. PowerPoint supports that directly in the Slide Show tab.

A) From Beginning (start at Slide 1)

Use this when:

- You want to deliver the full story in order.
- Your talk is timed and you want a clean start.
- You are recording the full presentation.

How to start:

- Slide Show tab → Start Slide Show group → From Beginning
- Shortcut: F5

Practical note:

- On some laptops, you may need Fn + F5 if your function keys control brightness/volume by default.

B) From Current Slide (start where you are editing)

Use this when:

- You are practicing a difficult slide and do not want to restart every time.
- You are presenting and you need to jump back into the show after a break.
- You are checking animations and transitions slide-by-slide.

How to start:

- Slide Show tab → From Current Slide
- Shortcut: Shift + F5

C) Custom Slide Show (present selected slides only)

This is one of the most professional features because it helps you present the right length for different situations without creating separate files.

Use this when:

- One group needs the "short version" (for example, 6 slides).
- Another group needs the "full version" (for example, 20 slides).
- You want to skip advanced slides for beginners, but keep them for Q&A.

How to use it (simple approach):

- Create your full deck first.
- Slide Show tab → Custom Slide Show → New
- Select the slides you want in that version
- Name it clearly (Example: "Short Version 6 Slides")
- Start the show using that custom list

Professional tip:

- Keep one master file. Use Custom Shows instead of maintaining two separate PowerPoint files that slowly drift apart.

2) Rehearsing and timing your talk

A good talk is not just "good slides." It is rhythm:

- Not too fast.
- Not too slow.
- Not stuck on one slide for five minutes.
- Not rushing the final slide because time is gone.

PowerPoint gives you a built-in rehearsal timer (commonly called Rehearse Timings) so you can practice with real numbers instead of guessing.

Why rehearsal timing matters

Rehearsal timing helps you:

- Learn your natural pace.
- Notice which slides are heavy and need simplification.
- Fit your message into the time you were given.
- Prepare for auto-advance shows (kiosk, self-running, recorded video).

How to rehearse timings (step-by-step)

1. Save your file first (so you do not lose work).
2. Slide Show tab → Rehearse Timings.
3. Start speaking as if the audience is present.
4. When you move to the next slide, PowerPoint records the time spent on the current slide.
5. At the end, PowerPoint asks if you want to keep the timings.

What to do with the results:

- If you are presenting live, you can still keep the timings as a learning record.
- If you want slides to advance automatically, you should keep timings and test the show again.

A practical timing rule for beginners

For a normal talk:

- Title slide: 10 to 20 seconds
- Most content slides: 40 to 70 seconds each
- Closing slide: 20 to 40 seconds

If a slide needs 2 minutes, it probably contains too much content. Fix the slide, not your breath.

Common mistakes during rehearsal

- Reading the slide word-for-word (slow and boring).
- Over-explaining one slide because it contains everything.
- Adding new points that are not on the slide and losing structure.
- Practicing only once and assuming you are ready.

A good habit:

- Rehearse once to discover problems.
- Adjust slides.
- Rehearse again to confirm the fix.

3) Recording narrations (when it helps)

Recording narrations can be excellent, but only when it serves a clear purpose. PowerPoint supports narration tools within the Slide Show workflow.

When narration is worth it

Record narrations when:

- You are sending the presentation to people who cannot attend live.
- You are building a training lesson for staff, students, or an online audience.
- You want a self-running presentation at a booth, office lobby, church event, or kiosk.
- You want to preserve a talk and reuse it later.

When narration is not worth it

Avoid narration when:

- You are presenting live and the room will hear you anyway.
- The topic changes often (your recording will become outdated quickly).
- The environment is noisy (bad audio ruins the value).
- You do not have time to record cleanly.

Recording checklist (simple and realistic)

Before you record:

- Use a quiet room.
- Test your microphone (even a basic headset often beats laptop mic).
- Close unnecessary apps to avoid notification sounds.

- Put your speaker notes in place so you do not forget your flow.

During recording:

- Speak slower than you think you should.
- Pause briefly after each key point.
- If you make a small mistake, keep going and re-record that slide later if needed.

After recording:

- Play back two or three slides to confirm audio quality.
- Check file size (audio can make files heavy).
- Consider exporting as a video if your goal is easy sharing.

Professional tip:

- A clean voice recording with simple slides often beats fancy animations with poor audio.

4) Setup group: show options, hiding slides, loop, pointer options

The Setup tools are what separate casual presenters from reliable presenters. They help you control how the show behaves: what the audience sees, what you see, whether the show loops, and whether some slides are hidden.

A) Set Up Slide Show (the control center)

In Set Up Slide Show, you can choose options like:

- How the show starts and ends

- Whether narration and animations play
- Whether the show loops
- Whether the audience can control navigation
- Which slides are included (all slides or a custom show)

This is where you prepare for real situations:

- A speaker-led presentation
- A self-running display
- A practice run with timings

B) Hiding slides (a smart professional trick)

Hidden slides are slides that remain in the file, but do not appear during the normal slideshow.

Use hidden slides for:

- Extra details for Q&A.
- Backup slides if someone asks for evidence.
- Advanced material that might not be needed.

How it helps:

- Your main show stays clean and short.
- You keep your deeper material without distracting the audience.

How to hide a slide:

- Select the slide thumbnail

- Right-click → Hide Slide (or use Slide Show tab options depending on version)
- The slide will show a small marker indicating it is hidden

Pro habit:

- Do not delete useful slides. Hide them and keep them for later.

C) Looping (for kiosks, booths, and self-running shows)

Looping is ideal when:

- Your deck runs at a booth, waiting room, or event stand.
- You want it to repeat continuously without a speaker.

If you loop a show:

- Keep it short.
- Keep text large.
- Use longer timing so people can read.
- Avoid fast transitions.

D) Pointer options (laser, pen, highlight)

During a slideshow, pointing is better than reading.

- Point to what matters.
- Let the audience look where you want them to look.

- Do not wave the mouse around like a nervous insect.

Common presenter controls:

- Laser pointer mode
- Pen or ink mode
- Highlighter mode
- Arrow cursor mode

Practical guidance:

- Use pointer tools for emphasis, not for decoration.
- If you draw on slides, practice first so your drawing is clean and not messy.

5) Monitors and Presenter View: single vs multiple screens

The Monitors group is small, but it changes everything for professional delivery. With Presenter View, the audience sees the slides, while you see your notes, your timer, and your next slide preview.

A) Single screen presentation (one laptop screen only)

When you only have one screen:

- You will usually present full-screen on the same display you control.
- You cannot privately see your notes unless you print them or use a second device.

How to succeed on one screen:

- Keep speaker notes short and readable.
- Memorize the flow of your slides.
- Use clear slide titles so you always know where you are.
- Practice your transitions between points.

B) Two screen setup (laptop + projector or external monitor)

This is the common professional setup:

- Audience: projector or external screen
- Presenter: laptop screen with Presenter View

What Presenter View typically gives you:

- Current slide
- Next slide preview
- Speaker notes
- Timer and elapsed time

If the wrong screen shows the wrong thing:

- Check Display Settings in Windows (Duplicate vs Extend).
- Extend is usually best for Presenter View.
- In PowerPoint, choose which monitor is the "Slide Show monitor."

Fast rescue move:

- If the audience is seeing your notes, stop immediately and fix it.

- Press Esc to exit slideshow, correct the display, then restart.

Calm truth:

- This happens even to experienced presenters. The difference is how fast they recover.

6) Key shortcuts for presenting (F5, Shift+F5, and more)

Keyboard shortcuts protect you when the mouse fails, the clicker fails, or you simply want speed. The Slide Show tab highlights the most important two: F5 and Shift+F5.

Here are practical shortcuts to learn early:

Starting and stopping

- F5: Start from beginning
- Shift + F5: Start from current slide
- Esc: End slideshow

Navigating slides

- Right arrow / Down arrow / Space: Next slide
- Left arrow / Up arrow / Backspace: Previous slide
- Type a slide number then press Enter: Jump to that slide (very useful when you must skip)

Screen control (simple but powerful)

- B: Black screen (pause attention on you)

- W: White screen (rarely needed, but useful sometimes)

Pointer tools (often used in live delivery)

- Right-click during slideshow to access Pointer Options (laser, pen, highlight)
- Press Esc to exit pointer mode if you accidentally start drawing

If you learn only three shortcuts for presenting, learn these:

- F5
- Shift + F5
- Esc

They keep you in control.

7) Practice project: Present like a pro in one short rehearsal

You are going to build and deliver a short deck, then improve it after one rehearsal. This is the fastest way to grow presentation skill.

Your assignment

Create a 6-slide deck, rehearse it once with timing, then adjust based on what the timing reveals.

Step A: Build a simple 6-slide deck

Use this structure (beginner-friendly and reliable):

1. Title slide
   - Title of talk

- Your name
- Date or audience

2. The problem (or the question)
- What is the issue?
- Why it matters?

3. Point 1
- One clear idea
- One example

4. Point 2
- One clear idea
- One example

5. Point 3
- One clear idea
- One example

6. Summary and next step
- 2 to 3 short takeaways
- One action you want the audience to take

Rules for this deck:
- Large text, minimal words.
- One idea per slide.
- No heavy animations.

- Simple transitions only, or none.

Step B: Prepare your presenter notes

For each slide, write 3 to 5 short lines in Notes.

- Not a full paragraph.
- Not a full script.
- Short prompts that keep you on track.

Example notes style:

- "Define the problem in one sentence."
- "Give one real example."
- "Ask one question to the audience."

Step C: Rehearse once and capture timing

Now run:

- Slide Show tab → Rehearse Timings (or use your version's rehearsal tool)

During rehearsal:

- Speak like the audience is real.
- Do not stop to fix slides.
- Finish the full 6 slides.

At the end:

- Accept saving timings (even if you will present live). The numbers will teach you where you are wasting time.

Step D: Adjust after one rehearsal (required)

Make at least three improvements based on what happened.

Here are the best improvements for beginners:

- If one slide took too long, split it into two slides or delete half the text.

- If you repeated yourself, reduce words and keep only the key line.

- If you rushed the final slide, shorten earlier slides.

- If you felt lost, rewrite slide titles so they guide you.

Then do one quick test:

- Start from current slide using Shift + F5 and confirm the hard slides feel easier now.

Step E: Deliver the deck

Deliver it in one of these ways:

- Present to a friend or colleague.

- Present to yourself while recording audio (optional).

- Present to an empty room, but take it seriously.

Your goal is not perfection.
Your goal is control:

- Smooth start.

- Steady pace.

- Clear transitions between ideas.

- Confident ending.

A final "presenter mindset" you should keep

PowerPoint is a tool. You are the presenter.

If the slides are perfect but you are nervous, the talk will feel weak.
If the slides are simple but you are clear and steady, the talk will feel strong.

Use Slide Show tools to practice and control delivery:

- Start correctly (F5, Shift+F5).
- Rehearse and learn your timing.
- Set up your show for the real room (hidden slides, looping when needed, pointer tools).
- Use Presenter View when you have two screens.

That is how you present like a pro.

PART NINE: REVIEW TAB (FIX, COLLABORATE, PROTECT)

The Review tab is where you slow down and make your presentation trustworthy. It helps you catch spelling and language issues, collect feedback through comments, and add basic protection so you can share your work without losing control.

In your book file, the Review tab is introduced as the place for Proofing, Comments, and Protection, with a reminder that some features can differ by system setup. It also explains the main purpose in simple terms: proofing helps you correct errors, comments help you collaborate, and protection helps you restrict editing permissions.

This chapter will rewrite that idea into a beginner-friendly, step-by-step method you can use every time.

1) Proofing group (spelling, language, research tools)

If your slides have spelling mistakes, people notice fast. It does not matter how good your ideas are. Errors weaken the message. Proofing tools help you polish your writing so your audience focuses on meaning, not mistakes.

Your file describes the Proofing group as a set of tools that helps you catch and fix spelling errors, look up word meanings online, and support multiple languages.

A) Spell check that actually works (the right way to use it)

PowerPoint can check spelling and grammar for your whole presentation, not only one slide. In many versions you can do this from the Review tab, and you can also press F7 to run spelling and grammar.

Practical habits that reduce mistakes:

1. Check spelling after you finish writing, not while you are still building slides.

2. Run the full check once near the end of your work.

3. Run it again after you copy text from email, PDF, or WhatsApp messages.

4. Pay attention to names, place names, and acronyms. Add correct terms to the dictionary only if you are sure they are correct.

Common spell check actions you will see:

- Ignore Once: skip one case

- Ignore All: skip every case of that word

- Change: fix one case

- Change All: fix every case of that word

- Add to Dictionary: tell PowerPoint this spelling is correct for the future

Beginner warning:
Do not "Add to Dictionary" for words that are actually wrong. That mistake can follow you into future presentations.

B) Language tools (set proofing language, avoid false errors)

If you write in more than one language, PowerPoint may mark correct words as wrong, because it is checking using the wrong language dictionary. The solution is not to ignore everything. The solution is to set the proofing language correctly.

Microsoft's guidance is clear: go to Review, then Language, then Set Proofing Language, and choose the correct language for the selected text.

Simple use cases:

- You are writing English slides but include Arabic names, French terms, or local language words.

- You are preparing a training deck for an audience that uses a different language.

- You copy text from another source and the proofing settings change.

Good beginner method:

1. Select the text that keeps being marked as wrong.

2. Review tab → Language → Set Proofing Language.

3. Choose the correct language.

4. If you do not want PowerPoint to check a special block of text (like code, product codes, or unusual terms), you can also choose "Do not check spelling or grammar" for that selected text.

Your file also highlights that PowerPoint supports multiple languages and can help you reach a wider audience by changing proofing language and grammar checking.

C) Research tools (when you are unsure about a word)

Your file mentions that PowerPoint can help you investigate word meanings online, which is useful when you face unfamiliar terms.

How to use this in real work:

- If you are writing a training deck and you are not sure you used the right word, look it up before you present.

- If you are using technical words (IT, health, finance), confirm meaning and spelling so you do not teach the wrong term.

- If you are writing for beginners, replace hard words with simple words where possible.

A for slides:
If a word needs a dictionary during a live talk, it probably should not be on the slide. Use a simpler word, then explain it with your voice.

D) Proofing for PowerPoint on eDrive or SharePoint)

If you use PowerPoint for the web, Microsoft explains that spelling, grammar, and style suggestions can appear as you type, and you can also run a "Check Slide" command from the Review tab.

What that means for you:

- If you collaborate online, you can still proof slides.

- Proofing can differ depending on where the file is stored (OneDrive, work or school, SharePoint).

- Always do a final check in the same place you will present from, especially if you will present using the desktop app.

E) Proofing checklist (quick and practical)

Before you share or present:

- Run spell check for the whole file.
- Confirm proofing language for any mixed-language slides.
- Fix repeated errors using Change All where appropriate.
- Avoid long sentences and crowded paragraphs. Slides are not essays.

2) Comments group (feedback workflow, navigating comments, deleting)

Comments are the safest way to collaborate because they let people speak into your work without rewriting it behind your back.

Your file explains that the Comments group works like Microsoft Word comments, allowing you to add and manage comments across the whole presentation. It also describes the core actions: New Comment, Show Markup, Previous Comment, Next Comment, and Delete Comment.

A) What comments are for (and what they are not for)

Use comments to:

- ask a question about a slide
- suggest a better phrase
- point out a missing step
- request a clearer example

- flag a slide that feels confusing or too long
- assign a task to someone (example: "Please confirm the date")

Do not use comments to:

- write your whole speech script inside the slide
- start side arguments that do not help the presentation
- dump long paragraphs that nobody will read

Beginner rule:
If a comment is longer than five lines, it probably should be a separate message (email or chat), or it should be split into smaller comments.

B) How to add a new comment

Your file says you can add comments by using the "New Comment" button in the Comments group, then typing into the comment box.

Simple steps:

1. Click the slide you want to comment on.
2. Click the object (text box, picture, chart) if you want the comment tied to that object.
3. Review tab → New Comment.
4. Type your note.
5. Save.

Good comment examples:

- "Slide 3: This title is too long. Can we shorten it to 5 words?"

- "Slide 4: Add a screenshot of the menu so beginners can follow."

- "Slide 5: Is te verify."

C) Show Markup (see all comment markers)

Your file notes that "Show Markup" highlights annotated scomments exist.

Why this matters:
If you have a 30-slide deck, you will not remember where comments are. Show Markup gives you a quick map of what needs attention.

Practical habit:
Before you finalize the deck, turn on markup and move through slides quickly to confirm you did not miss any comments.

D) Navigate comments (Previous and Next)

Your file explicitly mentions navigating using "Previous Comment" and "Next Comment." Microsoft's support also describes using Next and Previous in the Comments task pane.

Beginner workflow for cleaning up comments:

1. Open the comments pane.

2. Start at Slide 1.

3. Use Next to move through comments one by one.

4. For each comment, decide:

- o   apply the change nowon
- o   postpone and mark for later
- o   delete if it is no longer needed

E) Edit or delete comments (clean up the file)

Your file explains you can revise existing comments, and you can delete a comment by right-clicking it and selecting Delete Comment. Microsoft support also notes you can delete a comment from the comments pane.

Safe habits:

- Do not delete a comment until you have applied it or clearly rejected it.
- If the comment is important but you cannot act now, reply: "Noted. I will update after I confis finished, remove comments so your final file looks clean.

F) Comments as a respect tool (the "creative control" idea)

Your file makes an important point: feedback can be difficult when people impose changes without approval. It presents a better approach where collaborators propose suggestions, while the owner decides whether to accept or decline.

A simple rule that protects tosing. The slide owner decides.

This keeps collaboration friendly and keeps one clear voice in the deck.

3) Protection (what it means, when to use it, safe sharing habits)

Protection is not only about fear. It is about clarity: who can edit, who can view, and what happens when the file leaves your computer.

Your file describes Protection as securing important elements by restricting editing permissions, so you can share with confidence while keeping key details untouched. It also notes that some protection features may require licensing, a stable internet connection, and a subscription after a trial.

Let's make protection practical.

A) What protection can:

- require a password to open a presentation
- require a password to modify a presentation
- mark a presentation as final (read-only warning)
- restrict editing permissions for reviewers
- discourage accidental edits

Protection cannot:

- guarantee security if you share the password widely
- stop someone from taking screenshots or copying content in all cases
- stop editing if you only "mark as final" (people can still choose to edit anyway)

Microsoft is very clear that "Mark as Final" is not a security feature, because anyone can remove the final status and edit the file.

So you need to choose the right protection tool for the right need.

B) Password protection (open password vs modify password)

If your goal is to stop unauthorized people from opening the file, use encryoft's steps are: File → Info → Protect Presentation → Encrypt with Password, then save the file.

Two important warnings from Microsoft:

- Keep the password in a safe place.
- If you lose the password, it cannot be retrieved, and you may lose access to your own file.

If your goal is to let people open but not change, you can require a password to modify. Microsoft describes this using Save As, then Tools, then General Options, then "Password to modify."

Beginner recommendation:
For n unless absolutely necessary, because it can block smooth collaboration. If you must protect, consider "password to modify" or restsions.

C) Restrict access and permissions (for controlled collaboration)

Microsoft describes a "Restrict Access" path under Protect Presentation where you can assign read or change access to specific users.

This is often better than sending a file around on WhatsApp or email, because:

- you can limit who edits

- you can keep one master file online

- you reduce the risk of "ten versions" of the same deck

D) Mark as Final (useful signal, not a lock)

Mark as Final is a good way to tell your team: "This is the final draft, please do not edit."

Microsoft explains that it makes the file read-only and disables typing and proofing marks, but it can be undone easily, so it is not security.

Use Mark as Final when:

- you want to stop accidental edits
- you are sending the final deck to a supervisor
- you want to discourage last-minute rewriting

Do not rely on it when:

- the file contains sensitive material
- you truly need to stop editing

E) Safe sharing habits (simple rules that protect you)

Protection features help, but habits matter more. Here are safe habits that work even when you do not use passwords.

1. Keep a master copy
   Save one "Master" file that only you edit, and share copies for feedback.

2. Use clear file names
   Example:

- Training Deck v1 (Draft)
- Training Deck v2 (Comments Applied)
- Training Deck FINAL (No Comments)

3. Remove private notes before sharing
Presenter notes can contain private reminders, mistakes, or sensitive details. Before sharing widely, check notes on each slide.

4. Choose the right format
If the audience only needs to read, export to PDF. If they must reuse slides, share PPTX.

5. Share only with the right people
Microsoft's own guidance on protecting presentations includes the reminder to share access only with authorized people.

6. Do not put passwords in the same message as the file
If you email the file, send the password using a different method (text message or separate call).

4) Extra collaboration tool (optional): compare and accept or reject changes

Your file mentions "Track Changes" as part of the Review tab set of functions. In PowerPoint, this is commonly done using Compare, where you review changes and accept or reject edits.

Microsoft has a support article explaining "Track changes in your presentation," including accepting or rejecting changes and tips for working in the Comments task pane.

This is useful when:

- a reviewer made edits directly
- you want to approve changes one by one
- you need to preserve your original wording unless you accept an edit

Beginner advice:
If you are new to this, keep it simple. Use comments for suggestions first. Use compare only when someone already edited a copy and sent it back.

5) Practice project: share a file for feedback and apply changes using comments

Now you will practice the full Review tab method: proof, share, collect comments, apply changes, clean the deck, and protect the final copy.

Your project goal

You will:

- run a proofing check
- share your 6-slide deck with one reviewer
- collect at least 6 comments (about wording, layout, or clarity)
- apply changes
- remove resolved comments
- export or protect the final file

This is how real teams work.

Step 1: Prepare your deck (proof first)

1. Open your 6-slide deck.
2. Save a new copy:
   - "6-Slide Deck v1 (Review Draft)"
3. Run proofing:
   - Review tab → Spelling & Grammar, or press F7.
4. Check language settings for any mixed-language text:
   - Review → Language → Set Proofing Language.
5. Fix the obvious issues now, before you ask for feedback.

Reason:
You do not want reviewers wasting time on simple spelling errors you could have fixed in one minute.

Step 2: Decide what kind of feedback you want (be specific)

Do not say: "Please review." That invites random feedback.

Ask for 2 or 3 clear things, for example:

- "Please tell me if any slide title is unclear."
- "Please check if the steps are easy for beginners."
- "Please point out any slide with too much text."

This helps reviewers comment with purpose.

Step 3: Share the file for feedback (two safe methods)

Method A: Share a link (best for clean collaboration)

1. Upload the file to OneDrive or SharePoint (work or school).
2. Share with the reviewer as "Can comment" or "Can edit," depending on your needs.
3. Tell them: "Please use comments, not rewriting."

Method B: Send the file (simple when internet is limited)

1. Email the PPTX file.
2. Tell them to open it and add comments using Review → New Comment.
3. Ask them to return the same file with comments.

Step 4: Reviewer adds comments (what you tell them to do)

Send them these instructions:

1. Open the presentation.
2. Go to the slide you want to commx or object you mean.
3. Review tab → New Comment and type your note.
4. Use short, clear comments:
    - "Change this word to…"
    - "This step is missing…"
    - "Too much text here…"

Also tell them:

- Use Next and Previous to move through comment markers if needed.

Step 5: Apply feedback using a clean workflow

When you receive the commented file:

1. Save it as:
    - "6-Slide Deck v2 (Comments Received)"
2. Open the comments pane.
3. Turn on markup if needed, so you can see where comments exist.
4. Start at Slide 1 and use Next Comment to move comment by comment.
5. For each comment, choose one action:
    - Accept: make the change right away.
    - Clarify: reply with a question.
    - Reject: keep your original and reply politely with your reason.
6. After you act, delete the comment (or resolve it if your version supports resolving).
    - Your file describes deleting by right-clicking and choosing Delete Comment.

Keep going until no comments remain.

Step 6: Final proof after edits

After applying comments:

1. Run spelling and grammar again.
2. Check that slide titles still match what is on each slide.
3. Confirm you did not introduce new errors while rewriting.

Step 7: Protect or export the final version (choose the right finish)

Option A: Mark as Final (discourage edits)

- File → Info → Protect Presentation → Mark as Final.
  Remember: this discourages edits, but it is not security.

Option B: Encrypt with Password (stronger control)

- File → Info → Protect Presentation → Encrypt with Password.
  Store the password safely. If you lose it, Microsoft warns it cannot be recovered.

Option C: Export to PDF (best for "read only" sharing)

- Export as PDF if the audience only needs to view.

Beginner recommendation:
For training handouts or broad sharing, PDF is often the safest and simplest.

6) Quick problem fixes (common issues in real collaboration)

Problem: Reviewer edits slides directly instead of commenting

Fix:
Ask them to use comments next time. If they already edited, you can use Compare and accept or reject changes.

Problem: Too many comments become confusing

Fix:
Handle comments in order using Next and Previous, and delete resolved comments so the deck becomes clean again.

Problem: Spell check marks correct words as wrong

Fix:
Set the proofing language for that text.

Problem: You need to share but keep control

Fix:
Use restricted access or permission settings, or share as view-only when possible.

What you should carry forward

If you do three things from this chapter, do these:

1. Pro
2. Use comments for feedback, then apply changes in a controlled order.
3. Protect or export the final version based on the real need, not fear.

PART TEN: VIEW TAB (WORK FASTER AND STAY ORGANIZED)

The View tab is where PowerPoint becomes easier to manage, not just easier to decorate. Most beginners stay in one view, build slides, and then wonder why the presentation feels messy or hard to deliver. The View tab solves that by giving you different "work modes" for different jobs: writing the structure, editing slide content, checking flow, preparing speaker notes, and reviewing the deck like a viewer would.

In your book file, the View tab is described as a place to switch between **Normal view**, **Slide Sorter view**, **Notes Page view**, **Full Screen view**, and **Outline view**, each designed for a specific purpose. That is the right idea. This chapter rewrites it in a practical, beginner-first way, so you can work faster and keep control.

1) Normal view for building slides

What Normal view is

Normal view is your main workspace. It is the best view for creating and editing slides because it gives you three key areas at once:

- Slide thumbnails on the left (your slide list)
- The current slide in the middle (where you edit)
- The notes area below (where you can type speaker notes)

Microsoft describes Normal view as the editing mode you will use most often, with thumbnails on the left, the current slide in the main area, and a notes section beneath it.

Your file also highlights Normal view as the familiar default view when you enter a presentation.

When to use Normal view

Use Normal view when you are doing any of these:

- Adding new slides
- Typing titles and bullet poshapes
- Formatting text and objects
- Building charts, tables, and SmartArt
- Doing most of your day-to-day editing

How to work faster in Normal view

Here are habits that make Normal view feel "easy," even for large presentations:

1. Use the slide thumbnails like a table of contents
   Click any thumbnail to jump. Drag thumbnails to move slides. This is faster than scrolling through the main slide area.

2. Keep the slide titles meaningful
   A strong slide title acts like a signpost. When you are presenting or revising, the title quickly tells you what the slide is about. It also makes Slide Sorter and Outline view more useful later.

3. Use the notes area early, not at the end
   Beginners often add speaker notes only after

finishing slides. A better method is to add short notes while you build. This keeps your message clear and stops you from overcrowding slides.

4. Do not ignore the notes pane
In Normal view, the notes pane is right there for a reason. Microsoft notes that the notes pane sits beneath the slide window, and you can use it as cues for yourself while presenting.

A quick "Normal view discipline" rule

If you cannot explain the slide in one or two sentences in your notes, the slide is probably unclear. Fix the slide before you add design.

2) Outline view for structuring content

What Outline view is

Outline view is a text-first view that shows only the text on your slides, not pictures, charts, or shapes. Microsoft describes it as a view that displays only the text on your slides, making it useful for building an outline or storyboard.

Your file also names Outline view as a tool that helps you organize the presentation structure using a clear hierarchy.

Why beginners should care about Outline view

Outline view is where you fix the real problems that design cannot fix:

- Weak structure
- Repeated points
- Missing steps

- Confusing order
- Slides that do not match the talk

A presentation with strong structure can survive simple design. A presentation with weak structure collapses even with beautiful design.

When to use Outline view

Use Outline view when you want to:

- Plan the slials
- Write your full slide text quickly, then shorten it later
- Check whether your flow makes sense
- Rename slide titles in one pass so they are consistent
- Edit lots of text without clicking objects on slides

How to access Outline view (and why this matters)

Microsoft notes that in PowerPoint 2013 and later, Outline view is accessed from the View tab (not from Normal view the old way).

So if you cannot find it where someone else told you, do not panic. Go to the View tab.

Outline view rules that make your deck better

Here are simple rules that work in almost every topic:

1. Make slide titles talk like a teacher
   Bad title: "Security"
   Better title: "Security keeps your account safe"

Best title: "Use strong passwords and updates to stay safe"

2. Keep the outline balanced
If one point has 6 slides and the next has 1 slide, your talk will feel uneven. Either reduce the heavy part or expand the short part with one more supporting slide.

3. Delete repeated bullets
If you see the same bullet in two different slides, choose the best location and delete the duplicate.

4. Build the talk in your outline first
The outline should read like a clear message even without design.

Useful outline-related shortcuts (optional, but powerful)

Microsoft's PowerPoint shortcut guide includes tools that help with outline and pane navigation, like toggling between Outline and Thumbnails in Normal view.

Even if you do not memorize every shortcut, knowing that this exists helps you move faster over time.

3) Slide Sorter for reordering and flow

What Slide Sorter is

Slide Sorter view shows your slides as a grid of thumbnails so you can see many slides at once. Microsoft describes Slide Sorter as a view that displays all slides in rows so you can reorganize by dragging slides and even add sections to group slides.

Your file also describes Slide Sorter as the view that lets you arrange and reorder slides easily.

Why Slide Sorter is a "big deck" lifesaver

When you have 20, 40, or 80 slides, you cannot manage flow in Normal view well. Slide Sorter gives you the whole story on one screen.

Slide Sorter helps you:

- Spot the "too many slides on one topic" problem
- Spot missing transitions between sections
- Identify repeated slides or repeated messages
- Rearrange quickly without breaking design

When to use Slide Sorter

Use Slide Sorter when you want to:

- Reorder slides so the story makes sense
- Copy or move a group of slides together
- Delete slides that do not fit the main message
- Check pacing by looking at slide count per section
- Apply a transition style across many slides (carefully)

Practical workflow for reordering slides

Here is a simple method that works for beginners:

1. Switch to Slide Sorter view.

2. Read only the slide titles from left to right.

3. Ask: "If this was a speech, does the ord into a better order.

4. If two slides feel like one idea, combine or delete.

5. If a slide feels like it appears from nowhere, add a linking slide or move it.

Grouping with sections (simple organization)

Microsoft notes that in Slide Sorter view you can add sections to organize slides into meaningful groups.

Beginner use case:

- If you have a training deck, your sections might be "Basics," "Practice," "Common mistakes," and "Q&A."

Even if you never use sections, Slide Sorter alone will improve your flow.

4) Notes Page view for speaker notes

What Notes Page view is

Notes Page view is where you see a slide and its speaker notes in a printable layout, one slide per page with notes beneath it. Microsoft describes Notes Page view as a view where you can print notes or include notes in a presentation you send, or use them as cues for yourself.

Your file also calls Notes Page mode "perfect for previewing and editing speaker notes alongside corresponding slides."

Why notes matter (and how they protect your slides)

Speaker notes let you keep your slides clean.

A beginner mistake is turning slides into a full script. The result is tiny text, crowded slides, and a presenter who reads instead of teaches.

A better system is:

- Slides hold the key points.
- Notes hold the explanation.

When to use Notes Page view

Use Notes Page view when you want to:

- Write or revise speaker notes in a clean layout
- Prepare printed notes for yourself
- Check whether your talk fits your slides
- Confirm that your notes are readable and not too long

Notes Page view and safe sharing

Be careful with speaker notes when you share files.

Speaker notes may include:

- private reminders
- draft wording
- sensitive details
- jokes meant only for you

Before sending a deck to others, decide:

- Do they need the notes?
- Or should you export to PDF without notes?

That choice protects you.

A simple speaker notes template (beginner-friendly)

For each slide, use this format in your notes:

- One sentence: what this slide means
- One example: a real situation
- One question: what you want the audience to think about

This keeps notes short and usable.

5) Reading view vs full screen presng view is a full-screen style view designed for reviewing content, not for delivering a talk. A PowerPoint training manual describes Reading view as similar to Slide Show view, but it keeps the PowerPoint title band and system bars visible, unlike true Slide Show mode. (University of Pittsburgh Technology)

A simple way to think about it:

- Reading view is "watch the slides inside PowerPoint."
- Slide Show view is "present to an audience."

When Reading view is useful

Reading view is useful when:

- You want to review your deck quickly without editing
- You want to check visuals and spacing
- You are on one monitor and want a near full-screen preview
- You want to scan the deck without starting a full show

Full screen presenting

Full screen presenting normally means Slide Show view, where the presentation takes over the screen.

Your file references "Slide Show" as the setting that puts you into full-screen mode.

In earlier parts of your book, you also covered Slide Show tools, including presenter shortcuts like F5 and Shift+F5. (That continues to matter here because view choices and presenting choices are connected.)

Which one should beginners use?

Use Reading view for:

- private checking
- quick review

Use Slide Show (full screen) for:

- real presentation delivery
- rehearsal
- timing practice

- presenting to a group

A deck can look "fine" in Normal view but feel confusing in Slide Show. That is why you always test in a viewer-style mode before you call the deck finished.

6) Zoom and rulers, grids and guides (alignment help)

This part is where your slides start to look professional, even without advanced design. Most "messy slides" are not messy because of color. They are messy because objects do not line up.

Your file mentions a Show/Hide group that lets you show or hide items like rulers and gridlines. It also mentions a Zoom group that helps you magnify or reduce the slide view.

Let's turn that into a practical system.

A) Zoom (see what you are doing)

Why zoom matters

Zoom is not for decoration. Zoom is for control.

You zoom in when:

- you are aligning small objects
- you are placing icons, shapes, or labels
- you want to check spacing precisely

You zoom out whenslide

- you want to check balance and white space
- you want to confirm the slide is not crowded

Keyboard zoom shortcuts (simple and reliable)

Microsoft's support page on zooming applies to PowerPoint and Plus (+)**

- To zoom out: **Ctrl + Minus**

Your file also lists Ctrl + Plus for zoom in and Ctrl + Minus for zoom out.

Practical keyboard note:
On many keyboards, the plus sign is typed with Shift and the "=" key. So "Ctrl + Plus" may feel like "Ctrl + Shift + =" depending on your keyboard layout.

Fit to Window (the "reset" zoom)

Microsoft's zoom guidance also mentions **Fit to Window** in PowerPoint, which fits the slide to your current window size.

Fit to Window is what you use when:

- you zoomed in too far and got lost
- you want to check the whole slide quickly
- you want your slide to fill the available workspace neatly

align)

Rulers help you align objects with more discipline. If you care about cle can fix a lot.

Your file states that the Show/Hide group allows you to show or hide the ruler.

You can also toggle rulers using a keyboard shortcut. A PowerPoint keyboard shortcut reference from Microsoft includes ruler-related tools as part of view workflows and alignment aids, and an IndeZine tutorial specifically notes the ruler toggle shortcut as **Alt + Shift + F9**. (Indezine)

When to turn on rulers:

- when you are placing objects that must match across slides
- when you want even left and right margins
- when you want text boxes aligned to the same starting line

C) Gridlines (quick alignment guidance)

Gridlines are faint dotted lines that help you position objects evenly. They do not print. They are for building, not presenting.

Your file says the Show/Hide group lets you show or hide gridlines. xplicitly provides a shortcut to toggle gridlines: **Shift + F9**.

Microsoft's official keyboard shortcuts page also lists:

- Show or hide the grid: **Shift + F9**

That means the shortcut in your file matches common PowerPoint usage.

When to use gridlines:

- when placing multiple icons in a row
- when spacing shapes evenly

- when building simple diagrams
- when aligning tables and chart edges

D) Guides (the best tool for clean layout)

Guides are movable horizontal and vertical lines that you can drag to set your own alignment anchors. This is one of the easiest ways to make slides look tidy.

Microsoft's keyboard shortcuts list includes:

- Show or hide guides: **Alt + F9**

So if you want quick slide discipline, learn just these two:

- Alt + F9 (guides)
- Shift + F9 (gridlines)

How to use guides as a beginner:

1. Turn on guides.
2. Drag the vertical left margin line.
3. Drag the horizontal guide to create a consistent title baseline.
4. Align your text boxes and pictures to those guides across your deck.

Result:
Even simple slides suddenly look organized.

E) The "Show/Hide + Zoom" combo that makes you faster

Your file places Show/Hide and Zoom together for a reason.

Here is the practical combo:

- Zoom in to place objects precisely.
- Turn on guides to hold alignment.
- Turn on gridlines when you need equal spacing.
- Turn on ruler when you need consistent margins.
- Fit to Window when you want to review the full slide.

This combo is what turns "random placement" into "clean layout."

7) A simple "View Tab routine" for beginners

If you want one routine you can repeat for every presentation, use this:

Step 1: Outline vie strong slide titles.

- Arrange the story.
- Remove repeated text.

(Structu(Microsoft Support)

Step 2: Normal view (build slides)

- Insert content.
- Format text.
- Add visuals.
- Keep slides clean.

Normal view is your main editing workspace.

Step 3: Slide Sorter (check flow)

- Reorder slides.
- Remove weak slides.
- Ensure balance across sections.

Slide Sorter is designed for this kind of reordering.

Step 4: Notes Page view (prepare your talk)

- Add speaker notes.
- Keep your script off the slides.
- Make sure notes are readable.

Step 5: Reading view (quick review) or Slide Show (final check)

- Use Reading view for a fast preview.
- Use Slide Show for final rehearsal and real presenting.

This routine prevents the most common beginner pattern: Designing first, then discovering the message is unclear.

8) Practice project (based on your 6-slide deck)

You already have a 6-slide deck from earlier practice sections. Now you will use View tools to organize it and tighten delivery.

Practice goal

By the end of this practice, you will have:

- Better structure (Outline view)

- Better slide order (Slide Sorter)
- Better speaker notes (Notes Page)
- Cleaner alignment (Guides, gridlines, rulers)
- A final review in Reading view or Slide Show

Step A: Outline view cleanup (10 minutes)

1. Go to View tab → Outline view.
2. Read only the titles in order.
3. Rewrite titles so each title is a clear sentence or action.
4. Ret result:
   If someone reads only your outline, the talk still makes sense.

Step B: Slide Sorter flow check (10 minutes)

1. Switch to Slide Sorter view.
2. Look for these problems:
   - Two slides that are basically the same
   - A slide that feels out of place
   - Too many slides on one point
3. Drag slides to improve the order.
4. If needed, duplicate one slide and split its content into two simpler slides.

Microsoft describes Slide Sorter as ideal for reorganizing slides by dragging them.

Step C: Notes Page build (15 minutes)

1. Switch to Notes Page view.
2. For each slide, write:
    - one sentence meaning
    - one example
    - one question
3. Keep notes short enough that you can glance and speak naturally.

Microsoft explains Notes Page view supports notes that you can print or use as cues.

Step D: Alignment drill (10 minutes)

1. Go back to Normal view.
2. Turn on Guides (Alt + F9).
3. Turn on Gridlines (Shift + F9).
4. Turn on Ruler if you want tighter margins (Alt + Shift + F9).
5. On two slides, align:
    - titles to the same baseline
    - content boxes to the same left edge
    - pictures to the same size and position

Result:
Your deck starts to look consistent, even without changing the theme.

Step E: Reading view review (5 minutes)

1. Switch to Reading view.
2. Move through slides as a viewer.
3. Ask:
    - Does each title match what I see?
    - Is any slide too crowded?
    - Are images readable?

Reading view is designed for review in a near full-screen experience.

9) Shortcut box (View and organization essentials)

If you want to work faster, these are the shortcuts worth learning first.

- Alt + V: Jump to the View tab (your file mentions Alt + V for View access).
- Ctrl + Plus (+): Zoom in
- Ctrl + Minus (-): Zoom out
- Shift + F9: Toggle gridlines
- Alt
- Alt + Shift + F9: Toggle rulers
- Ctrl + Shift + Tab: Toggle between Outline and Thumbnail views in Normal view
- F5: Start slideshow from beginning

- Esc: Exit slideshow and return to editing (your file also mentions Esc as a quick return key).

You do not need all of them today. Start with: Guides, Gridlines, Zoom, and Slide Sorter.

10) Common problems and quick fixes

Problem: "My slides look fine, but feel confusing when I present."

Fix:
Use Slide Sorter to review the flow and remove weak slides. Check in Slide Show view and rehearse.

Problem: "My slide objects are never aligned."

Fix:
Turn on Guides and Gridlines. Use them as anchors, not decoration.

Problem: "My slides are too crowded."

Fix:
Use Reading view or Slide Show view to see the deck like an audie
Then shorten bullets and move explanation into speaker notes.

Problem: "I cannot find Outline view."

Fix:
Go to the View tab. Microsoft notes that in newer versions, Outline view is accessed from the View tab.

What you should carry forward

The View tab is not extra. It is your control panel for order and speed.

- Normal view builds slides.

- Outline view builds the message.

- Slide Sorter builds the flow.

- Notes Page builds the talk.

- Reading view checks what a viewer will experience.

- Zoom, rulers, gridlines, and guides build clean al

Next section is usually PART ELEVEN: SLIDE MASTER AND CONSISTENCY (how to control fonts, layouts, and repeated design elements across the whole deck) which your file also points to through Slide Master and related master views.

PART ELEVEN: OTHER HIDDEN TABS AND POWER FEATURES

PowerPoint looks simple at first because you mainly see the usual Ribbon tabs such as Home, Insert, Design, Animations, Slide Show, Review, and View. But PowerPoint has extra tabs that only appear when you select certain objects. These are often called "hidden tabs" because you do not see them until you click a picture, a shape, a table, a chart, or SmartArt. Your guide already flags these as "Other Hidden Tabs" in the contents and treats them as a key skill area.

In this part, you will learn what these tabs are, how to make them appear on purpose, and how to use them like a pro. These tabs save time because they collect the exact tools you need for the selected item, instead of forcing you to hunt through menus. And once you master them, you can build slides faster, keep your design consistent, and produce handouts that look like you planned them from the start.

What "hidden tabs" means and how they appear (contextual tabs)

What they are

PowerPoint's Ribbon is organized into tabs, and each tab holds groups of tools. Your guide explains that tabs sit on the Ribbon and the Ribbon contains the command buttons for tasks.

A "hidden tab" is simply a tab that appears only when it is needed. Microsoft calls these contextual tabs (sometimes written as "context tabs" in class notes). They show up when you select an object that has special formatting options.

How they appear

They appear in one of these common ways:

1. You click an object on the slide (picture, shape, table, chart, SmartArt).

2. You insert an object, and PowerPoint selects it automatically.

3. You select the object using a tool like Selection Pane (useful when objects overlap).

The moment the object is selected, PowerPoint adds one or more extra tabs on the Ribbon. When you click away to empty space, those tabs disappear again.

How to recognize them quickly

Contextual tabs usually have:

- A name tied to the object (Picture Format, Shape Format, Table Design, Chart Design, SmartArt Design).

- A colored label area above the tab name (depending on your version of PowerPoint).

A simple habit that prevents confusion

When you feel "lost" in PowerPoint, do this:

- Click the object you want to change.

- Look at the Ribbon again.

- If a special tab appears, that is where the best tools will be.

This one habit fixes many beginner problems, especially "Why can't I crop?" or "Where is table formatting?" or "How do I change this chart style?"

Working with pictures and shapes Format tabs

Pictures and shapes are everywhere in presentations. The biggest difference between an average slide and a professional slide is often how well pictures and shapes are formatted.

Picture tools (Picture Format tab)

How to open it

1. Insert a picture: Insert tab → Pictures (or drag and drop an image onto the slide).
2. Click the picture.
3. The Picture Format tab appears.

The most useful picture tools (the ones that save you real time)

1) Crop properly (and stop fighting with image sizes)

- Click the picture → Picture Format → Crop.
- Drag the black crop handles to cut the image.
- Click Crop again to apply.

Pro tip: Use crop to keep images consistent across slides. Instead of stretching an image (which looks cheap), crop it.

2) Remove Background (when you need a clean cut-out)

- Click the picture → Remove Background.
- Adjust selection markers.
- Keep Changes.

This is powerful when you want a person, logo, or object on top of a clean slide background.

3) Corrections and Color
If your photo is too dark or too bright:

- Corrections lets you adjust brightness and sharpness quickly.
- Color lets you adjust saturation and tone.

Use these lightly. A small correction can make an image look "new," but too much makes it look fake.

4) Compress Pictures (reduce file size)
Large pictures make your PowerPoint file heavy, slow, and hard to share.

- Picture Format → Compress Pictures.
- Choose a resolution that fits your goal (projector vs email vs print).

If your presentation is meant for sharing on WhatsApp, email, or low bandwidth, this tool matters.

5) Align, Distribute, and Position
When you have multiple pictures:

- Select them (hold Shift and click each).

- Picture Format → Align (align left, center, right, top, middle, bottom).

- Use Distribute Horizontal or Distribute Vertical.

This is one of the fastest ways to make your slide look "designed" rather than "random."

6) Order: Bring Forward / Send Backward
Pictures and shapes often overlap.

- Use Bring Forward / Send Backward to control which item is on top.

If your text disappears behind a photo, it is usually an order issue, not a "missing text" issue.

7) Group and Ungroup
If you built a layout with a photo, a caption, and a shape background:

- Select all items → Group.
  Now they move together as one unit.

This makes your slide editing much easier.

Shape tools (Shape Format tab)

How to open it

1. Insert a shape: Insert tab → Shapes → choose a shape.

2. Draw it on the slide.

3. Click the shape.

4. The Shape Format tab appears.

The shape tools that make your slides look professional

1) Shape Fill, Shape Outline, Shape Effects
These three options are your core shape controls:

- Shape Fill changes the inside color.
- Shape Outline changes the border.
- Shape Effects adds shadow, glow, soft edges, and 3D effects.

A common pro habit is to use simple fills and light shadows, not heavy 3D.

2) Edit Shape
This lets you change a shape into another shape without deleting it.

- Example: Turn a rectangle into a rounded rectangle.
- Example: Change a basic arrow into a block arrow.

3) Merge Shapes (advanced but powerful)
In some PowerPoint versions, you can merge shapes to create custom graphics:

- Union, Combine, Fragment, Intersect, Subtract.

This is how you create clean icons and custom designs without external software.

4) Align and Distribute
Same principle as pictures:

- Align edges, align centers, distribute spacing evenly.

5) Rotate and Flip
Use rotate for angled banners, diagonal labels, or creative layout lines.

6) Format Shape Pane
Right-click a shape → Format Shape.
This opens a detailed pane with precise controls:

- Transparency
- Gradient fills
- Line styles
- Shadow settings
- Size and properties

If you want exact control, this pane is better than clicking random presets.

Table tools and Chart tools

Tables and charts often trigger two tabs (sometimes more), because they have both design and layout needs.

Table tools (Table Design and Layout tabs)

How to open them

1. Insert a table: Insert tab → Table.
2. Click inside the table.
3. You will see Table Design and Layout tabs.

Table Design tab: make tables readable fast

Key tools:

- Table Styles: apply a clean style quickly.
- Shading: add background color to header row or key rows.
- Borders: control where lines appear.

Pro habit: Avoid heavy borders everywhere. Use fewer lines, and let spacing do the work.

Common best practice for beginner-friendly slides:

- Bold header row
- Light fill on header row
- Minimal border lines
- Enough padding (space inside cells)

Layout tab: control cells like a spreadsheet

Key tools:

- Insert Rows/Columns
- Delete Rows/Columns
- Merge Cells (combine two cells into one)
- Split Cells (break one cell into multiple)
- Cell Alignment (top-left, center, bottom-right, etc.)
- Distribute Rows / Distribute Columns (even spacing)

Power move: Use "Distribute Columns" after you edit column widths manually. It instantly restores order.

Chart tools (Chart Design and Format tabs)

Charts are not just "Insert and done." Charts are a mini system inside PowerPoint.

How to open them

1. Insert a chart: Insert tab → Chart.
2. PowerPoint opens an Excel-like data sheet.
3. After inserting, click the chart.
4. You will see Chart Design and Format tabs.

Chart Design tab: build the chart correctly

Key tools:

- Add Chart Element: titles, labels, legend, gridlines.
- Quick Layout: fast layout presets.
- Change Colors: apply a matching color set.
- Chart Styles: choose a clean look.
- Switch Row/Column: fixes wrong chart orientation.
- Select Data / Edit Data: adjust what the chart shows.

Pro habit: Make sure your chart answers one question clearly. If the audience needs you to explain the chart for five minutes just to understand it, the chart is too busy.

Format tab: make it match your slide design

Key tools:

- Format Selection: choose a part of the chart and format it.

- Shape Fill / Outline / Effects: style chart areas.

- WordArt Styles: style chart text.

- Arrange: align, bring forward, send backward (yes, charts can overlap too).

- Size: exact chart dimensions.

Power move: Format one chart perfectly, then copy and paste it to other slides and just edit the data. This keeps your charts consistent.

SmartArt tools

SmartArt is PowerPoint's fast way to create diagrams that look clean without you drawing everything manually.

How to open SmartArt tools

1. Insert tab → SmartArt.

2. Pick a category (List, Process, Cycle, Hierarchy, etc.).

3. Insert it.

4. Click the SmartArt.

5. You will see SmartArt Design and Format tabs.

SmartArt Design tab: structure and meaning

Key tools:

- Add Shape: add new boxes or steps.

- Promote / Demote: change hierarchy (very useful for org charts).
- Move Up / Move Down: rearrange order.
- Layouts: switch diagram type while keeping text.
- Change Colors: apply a color scheme quickly.
- SmartArt Styles: polished looks with one click.
- Reset Graphic: remove custom formatting and return to default.

Power move: Use the Text Pane (usually on the left side) to type and organize quickly. It is faster than clicking each shape.

SmartArt Format tab: fine styling

Key tools:

- Change Shape
- Shape Fill / Outline / Effects
- WordArt and text formatting
- Align and distribute
- Size controls

Pro habit: Keep SmartArt simple. Use it for structure, not decoration.

Notes and handouts tools

Notes and handouts separate presenters from "people who just click next."

Speaker Notes (for the presenter)

Speaker notes allow you to write what you will say, without crowding your slide with text.

Ways to use notes well:

- Put key points you must not forget.
- Put short stories or examples you want to tell.
- Put stats and numbers you may need during Q and A.
- Put reminders like "pause here" or "ask the audience."

Where to view notes:

- Normal view: notes area under the slide.
- Notes Page view: a full page with slide plus notes.

Presenter View (best for live presenting)

Presenter View shows:

- Current slide
- Next slide preview
- Notes
- Timer and controls

This is ideal when you have a projector for the audience and a laptop screen for yourself.

Handouts (for the audience)

Handouts are printed pages that contain multiple slides per page, with or without note lines.

Common handout layouts:

- 1 slide per page (big and readable)
- 2 slides per page (common for training)
- 3 slides per page with lines (best for note-taking)
- 6 slides per page (compact)
- 9 slides per page (tiny, only for reference)

Handouts are very useful for:

- Workshops
- Church teaching sessions
- School lessons
- Meetings where people need to write notes

Optional advanced topics that help a lot

These are not "extra for fun." These are tools that quickly raise your work level.

Selection Pane (control overlapping objects)

When a slide has many items, clicking the right one becomes hard.

Use:

- Home tab or Format tab → Select → Selection Pane (location depends on version)

What it gives you:

- A list of all objects on the slide.
- Ability to rename objects (like "Title box," "Photo 1," "Logo").
- Eye icons to hide objects temporarily.

This is one of the cleanest ways to edit busy slides.

Guides, Gridlines, and Snap

If your alignment feels slightly off, turn on visual helpers:

- View tab → Guides / Gridlines (depending on version)

These help you place objects evenly and avoid "almost aligned" layouts.

Reuse Slides (build faster across decks)

If you have a good slide in an old file, reuse it instead of rebuilding:

- Insert → Reuse Slides (or Home → New Slide dropdown → Reuse Slides, depending on version)

This is a big time saver when you teach the same topic many times.

Format Painter (keep styles consistent)

Your guide already teaches Format Painter early because it saves time across Office apps. The same idea helps in PowerPoint:

- Copy a text style, shape style, or formatting and apply it elsewhere.

Consistency is what makes slides look intentional.

Slide Master basics (consistent design)

Slide Master is where you control your whole presentation design from one place.

What Slide Master is

Slide Master is a special editing mode where you set:

- Fonts
- Colors
- Backgrounds
- Placeholder positions
- Header/footer placement
- Logo placement
- Layout rules

When you do this once in Slide Master, every slide that uses that layout follows the same style.

When you should use Slide Master

Use Slide Master when:

- You want all slides to have the same title position.
- You want a logo on every slide.
- You want consistent footer text (organization name, date, page numbers).

- You want your presentation to look like one unit, not separate slides.

How to open Slide Master

1. Go to the View tab.

2. Click Slide Master.

3. The left panel changes to master layouts.

4. Edit the top master (affects all layouts) or a specific layout (affects only that type).

What to change first (the safest order)

1. Set theme fonts and theme colors (so your whole deck matches).

2. Add logo and footer information if needed.

3. Adjust title and content placeholders.

4. Check at least three slides (title slide, content slide, section header slide) before you close Master view.

How to exit Slide Master

- Click Close Master View.

Power rule: Do not manually format every slide to "fix" design problems. Fix the master, then let slides follow it.

Handouts and printing setup

Printing is where many PowerPoint users get surprised, because what you see on screen is not always what prints well.

Print settings you should know

When you go to File → Print, you can usually choose:

1. **What to print**

   - Slides (full page)
   - Notes Pages (slide with speaker notes)
   - Handouts (multiple slides per page)
   - Outline (text-only outline)

2. **Slides per page (handout layout)**

   - 2, 3, 4, 6, or 9 slides per page
   - 3 slides per page often includes lines for notes

3. **Color settings**

   - Color (best but expensive)
   - Grayscale (good balance)
   - Pure black and white (best for cheap printing, but some designs may lose meaning)

4. **Hidden slides**
   You can often choose whether to print hidden slides. This matters if you hid "extra" slides meant only for Q and A.

5. **Scaling**
   Look for settings such as:

   - Fit to page
   - Scale to fit paper

This prevents slides from being cut off at the edges.

Export to PDF (best for sharing and printing)

If your goal is to send handouts to someone else, exporting to PDF is often the safest route because it locks the layout.

Common use cases:

- Sending training materials to students
- Printing in a cyber café
- Sharing with a church team on WhatsApp

A strong workflow for training handouts

If you teach regularly, do this:

1. Build your slides using Slide Master so design stays consistent.
2. Write speaker notes under each slide (short, clear points).
3. Choose Handouts, 3 slides per page with lines for the audience.
4. Export that handout view to PDF for sharing.

This workflow makes you look prepared, even when you are teaching a topic for the first time.

A quick practice assignment (to lock these skills in)

If you want these tabs to become normal to you, practice like this:

1. Create a new blank presentation.
2. Insert one picture, one shape, one table, one chart, and one SmartArt.

3. Click each item and watch which hidden tabs appear.

4. For each item, do at least three actions from its special tab:
    - Picture: crop, compress, align
    - Shape: fill, outline, effects
    - Table: style, merge cells, align text
    - Chart: change layout, add data labels, change colors
    - SmartArt: add shape, change layout, change colors

5. Go to View → Slide Master and add a simple footer text.

6. Print preview a 3-slides-per-page handout and export to PDF.

Do this once, slowly, and you will feel the difference the next time you build a real presentation.

PART TWELVE: KEY TERMINOLOGIES AND QUICK HELP

This section is your "rescue kit" for two situations that happen to every beginner:

1. You hear a computer or PowerPoint term and you are not sure what it means.

2. Something goes wrong in your presentation and you need a fast fix.

Your book already includes a computing terminologies glossary in alphabetical order, including terms like "Compressing," "Default," "Download," "Drag," "Driver," "Encrypt," "Executable files," and more. It also introduces core PowerPoint interface terms such as Title bar, Status bar, Quick Access Toolbar, tabs, and Ribbon.

In this rewritten Part Twelve, you will get:

- A clean glossary (based on your file, plus the most useful PowerPoint workspace terms from your earlier chapters).

- Common mistakes and fixes, written like a real troubleshooting guide.

- A quick checklist before presenting, so you do not get embarrassed by avoidable problems.

Also, remember the simplest troubleshooting habit in PowerPoint: click the object first. Many "missing tools" appear only when the object is selected, which your book explains through "hidden tabs" and the Format tab behavior.

A) Glossary of key terms (as used in your book)

1) PowerPoint workspace terms (the ones you will hear every day)

These terms appear repeatedly in your book when describing the PowerPoint window and how the program is organized.

Term	What it means in simple words	Why it matters
Ribbon	The strip at the top that holds tabs and command buttons. Your book calls it the area that contains command buttons needed for each task.	If you know where to look on the Ribbon, you stop guessing.
Tab	A category on the Ribbon (Home, Insert, Design, and so on). Your book lists these as the main PowerPoint tabs.	Tabs organize tools by task.
Group	A cluster of related tools inside a tab (Font group, Paragraph group, etc.). Your book explains that groups appear under tabs like Home.	Helps you find tools faster instead of scanning the whole tab.
Quick Access Toolbar	A small toolbar for your favorite commands (often Save, Undo, Redo). Your book lists it among the main bars.	Saves time when you repeat actions.
Title bar	The top bar that shows the	Helps you

Term	What it means in simple words	Why it matters
	file name and PowerPoint window controls. Your book identifies it as one of the key bars.	confirm which file you are editing.
Status bar	The bar at the bottom that shows slide info and view/zoom controls. Your book includes it among key bars.	Lets you move faster (view changes and zoom).
Slide pane / Thumbnails	The left side where small slide previews appear. Your book describes a slide pane as part of the main window features.	Best way to reorder slides quickly.
Workspace / Slide area	The big center area where you edit the current slide. Your book refers to the "central work area."	This is where your content is built.
Contextual tabs (hidden tabs)	Tabs that appear only when you select an object (picture, table, chart, SmartArt). Your book calls these "other Hidden tabs," and also explains the Format tab appears when items are selected.	If you do not know this, you will feel like features are missing.

One key idea from your file: the tabs and Ribbon are not decorations. They are the control center for every action you take.

2) Computing terminologies glossary (from your file)

Below are the glossary terms from your book, rewritten in cleaner beginner language while keeping the original meaning and focus.

Term	Meaning (simple)	Practical example in PowerPoint work
Compressing	Reducing file size so it takes less space and is easier to send.	Compress pictures or media so your PPTX can be emailed.
Default	A ready-made setting already chosen for you.	Default slide size is often Widescreen unless you change it.
Download	Copying a file from another computer or the internet to your computer.	Download a template or a font before building a deck.
Drag	Moving something by holding the mouse button and moving the mouse.	Drag slide thumbnails to reorder your presentation.
Driver	Software that helps hardware work with your computer.	A projector might not display well if the display driver is outdated.

Term	Meaning (simple)	Practical example in PowerPoint work
Encrypt	Scrambling information so only someone with the right key can read it.	Encrypt sensitive files before sharing in public spaces.
Executable files	Files that start a program, often ending with .exe.	Installing PowerPoint add-ins often uses an executable installer.
File name extension	Characters at the end of a filename that show file type.	.pptx for PowerPoint, .pdf for exported handouts.
File types	Formats of files, shown by extensions, indicating what program opens them.	A .pptx opens in PowerPoint, not in Excel.
Filter	Showing only items that meet criteria, without deleting.	Filter your folder view to show only PowerPoint files.
Gadget	A small program/tool for quick info or features.	Less common today, but the idea is "small tools that do one job."
Icon	A small picture that represents a file, folder,	PowerPoint's icon helps you spot

Term	Meaning (simple)	Practical example in PowerPoint work
	or program.	.pptx files quickly.
Importing	Copying photos, music, or videos from a device to your computer.	Import photos from your phone, then insert into slides.
Library	A collection of files/folders gathered from locations.	Your Pictures library can be a source for slide images.
Location	A place where files can be stored (drive, folder, etc.).	Save your presentation in a known folder you can find again.
Malicious software (malware)	Software designed to harm your computer.	Avoid unknown "free templates" that come with unsafe installers.
Memory (RAM)	Temporary working memory for running programs.	Heavy slides with big videos can slow PowerPoint on low RAM PCs.
Navigation pane	Left area in a folder window showing drives and folders.	Use it to quickly open your PowerPoint folder before class.

Term	Meaning (simple)	Practical example in PowerPoint work
Network	Devices connected to share data (wired or wireless).	Your school network might block online videos during presentation.
NTFS	A Windows file system that supports features like file compression.	Large PPTX files store more reliably on NTFS drives than older formats.
Pointing	Moving the pointer to a position using mouse/pen.	Point at buttons during Slide Show to trigger actions/links.
Program (application)	Instructions that perform tasks, also called software.	PowerPoint is the program used to build slides.
Public folder	A Windows folder for sharing files on the same PC/network.	Place a deck there if multiple users need it on one computer.
Removable media	Storage you can insert/remove (USB, CD, memory card).	Carry your final PPTX and a PDF backup on a USB drive.
Rights	Policies controlling access to	You may not have rights to install

Term	Meaning (simple)	Practical example in PowerPoint work
	computer/network resources.	fonts on a work computer.
Saved searches	Searches you save so you can run them again.	Save a search for ".pptx" inside your training materials folder.
Shortcut	A link to a program/file placed for quick access.	Put a PowerPoint shortcut on the desktop for quick launching.
Sound card	Hardware for recording and playing sound.	Audio in slides may fail if sound drivers are broken.
Tablet pen	A pen used to interact with items on screen.	Useful for annotation during teaching if you present on a tablet.
Tags	Custom file properties used to help organize files.	Add tags like "Training" or "Church" to find decks faster.
Taskbar	The desktop area with Start button and open programs.	When presenting, keep distractions off the taskbar if possible.

Term	Meaning (simple)	Practical example in PowerPoint work
Themes	A set of colors and styles (your file defines this broadly).	In PowerPoint, themes keep fonts/colors consistent across slides.

That glossary is not only "computer theory." It directly improves how you save, share, protect, and troubleshoot PowerPoint files.

B) Common mistakes and fixes (fast troubleshooting)

This section is written so you can fix problems in minutes, even under pressure.

1) Text not fitting on the slide

What you see

- Words overflow outside the text box.
- Bullet points become too small.
- Lines disappear at the bottom of the placeholder.

Why it happens

- You typed more text than the placeholder can hold.
- AutoFit shrinks the text automatically to force it to fit.
- The text box is too small for the font size you chose.

Microsoft explains that AutoFit Text is the default behavior: if you add more text than can fit, PowerPoint reduces font size.

Fast fixes (choose the best one)

Fix A: Split text into another slide (best for clarity)
PowerPoint can split the body text into two slides. Microsoft describes "Split Text Between Two Slides" as a tool that creates a new slide and divides text roughly in half. Use it when your slide has too many bullets.

Fix B: Reduce your text (best for beginners)

- Keep one idea per slide.

- Convert long sentences into short bullets.

- Move explanations into speaker notes.

This is not just style. It prevents unreadable slides.

Fix C: Resize the placeholder

- Click the text box border.

- Drag the handles to make it bigger.

- Keep margins consistent (do not stretch randomly).

Fix D: Control AutoFit
If AutoFit is making your text too small, change the fitting setting:

- Use "Stop Fitting Text" so PowerPoint does not keep shrinking it. Microsoft lists "Stop Fitting Text" as an option that stops resizing and lets text overfill the box, so you can fix overflow another way.

Prevention habit

Write slide titles and bullets in Outline view first, then shorten them before adding design. This reduces overflow problems later.

2) Images too large (or slides become messy after inserting pictures)

What you see

- The image covers your text.
- The file becomes slow after inserting a few photos.
- The slide looks "heavy" and crowded.

Why it happens

- Phone camera photos are often very high resolution.
- PowerPoint keeps image editing data by default.
- You inserted large images without resizing or cropping.

Fast fixes

Fix A: Resize correctly

- Click the picture.
- Drag a corner handle (not a side handle) to keep proportions.
- Use Align tools to position it neatly.

Fix B: Crop instead of stretching
Cropping removes unwanted parts and keeps the image looking clean.

Fix C: Reduce overall file size through PowerPoint settings
Microsoft recommends steps that reduce PowerPoint file size, including:

- Discard editing data (removes stored data used to restore images).

- Ensure "Do not compress images in file" is not selected.

- Lower default resolution (for example 150 ppi or lower).

This single change can rescue a presentation that has become too large or too slow.

Prevention habit

Before inserting images, decide what the image must show. Then crop early. A cropped image is usually clearer than a full photo squeezed into a slide.

3) Fonts changing on another computer

What you see

- Your text looks different on another laptop.

- Spacing changes and slides break.

- Lines wrap differently.

Why it happens

If the other computer does not have the fonts you used, PowerPoint substitutes an available font. Microsoft explains that missing fonts cause substitution, and recommends using common fonts like Arial and Times New Roman for best compatibility.

Also, some third-party fonts cannot be embedded because of licensing rights, which can cause problems when sharing with others.

Fast fixes

Fix A: Use common fonts
If you know the presentation will be used on unknown computers, use fonts that exist almost everywhere (Arial, Calibri, Times New Roman).

Fix B: Embed fonts (when you must preserve your look)
Microsoft's file-size guidance includes instructions for embedding fonts:

- File > Options > Save
- Select "Embed fonts in the file"
- Choose "Embed only the characters used in the presentation" to limit file size.

Important: embedding fonts can increase file size, so use it when design consistency matters.

Fix C: Test on the target computer
The most honest solution is simple: open the file on the computer you will use for presenting. If it breaks, you have time to fix it.

Prevention habit

If you teach or train in many places, build a "safe font template" and reuse it for most presentations.

4) Video not playing (or cannot be inserted)

What you see

- The video refuses to insert.
- The video inserts but does not play.
- Audio plays but video is black.
- Video plays on your laptop but fails on the projector computer.

Why it happens

Video playback depends on format and codecs. Microsoft recommends:

- Video: .mp4 encoded with H.264 video and AAC audio for best compatibility across Windows and Mac versions of PowerPoint.
- Audio: .m4a encoded with AAC audio.

Microsoft also lists supported formats, including .mp4, .m4v, .mov, .wmv, .avi (some need extra codecs), and others.

Fast fixes

Fix A: Convert the video to the recommended format
If your video is not in a friendly format, convert it to:

- .mp4 (H.264 + AAC)

This is often easier than trying to solve a codec mystery.

Fix B: If it is a codec issue
Microsoft notes that if a supported format will not play, you may need a missing codec or you can convert the file to the recommended format, and conversion is often easier.

Fix C: Keep a backup plan
For high-stakes presentations:

- Carry the video file separately on a USB.

- Also carry a PDF version of your slide deck (in case video fails, you can still teach).

Prevention habit

Test the video on the same computer and environment you will use for presenting, including speakers and projector.

5) File too big (hard to send, slow to open, crashes)

What you see

- You cannot email the file.

- The file takes long to open.

- PowerPoint freezes while saving.

- Sharing on WhatsApp fails.

Why it happens

The biggest causes are:

- Large images

- Embedded fonts

- Embedded video/audio
- Stored editing data

Microsoft's "Reduce file size" guidance recommends:

- Discard editing data
- Compress images (ensure "Do not compress images" is off)
- Lower default resolution
- Embed only characters used if embedding fonts is needed.

Fast fixes

Fix A: Compress and lower image quality
Use the settings above (discard editing data, compress images, lower resolution).

Fix B: Reduce embedded fonts
If you embedded fonts, choose "Embed only the characters used."

Fix C: Replace heavy media
If a video makes the file huge, consider:

- linking to the file externally (advanced)
- replacing the video with a screenshot and a short explanation
- using a shorter clip

Prevention habit

Treat file size as part of planning. If you know you will send the deck over weak internet, build with smaller images from the start.

6) Links not working (hyperlinks and action buttons)

What you see

- Clicking does nothing during Slide Show.
- Links open the wrong file or break on another computer.
- Internal navigation (Back, Home) fails.

Why it happens

- The link points to a file path that does not exist on the new computer.
- You are trying to click a hyperlink while editing without using the proper method.
- Action button settings were not tested.

Fast fixes

Fix A: Test hyperlinks the right way
Microsoft states you can test hyperlinks during editing by right-clicking and choosing "Open Hyperlink," and also advises testing in Slide Show before presenting to ensure they work.
Microsoft also confirms you can test links by right-clicking and selecting Open Hyperlink.

Fix B: For internal navigation, use action buttons carefully
Microsoft explains action buttons as shapes you insert, then

assign actions like "Hyperlink to next slide, previous slide, first slide," and more.

Fix C: Avoid linking to files that will not travel with you

If you link to a local file on your laptop, it likely breaks when moved. If you must use external files, keep them in the same folder and move the folder as one unit.

Prevention habit

Before presenting, run Slide Show and click every link once. Do not assume.

C) Quick checklist before presenting (your last 5 minutes)

This checklist matches your outline goals and adds a few high-impact checks that prevent common failures.

1) Fonts readable

- Titles are large enough to read from the back of the room.
- Body text is not tiny.
- You did not rely on all-caps or heavy italics.

Microsoft's accessibility guidance recommends using familiar fonts and avoiding excessive italics or underlines because it increases reading load.

2) Contrast ok

- Dark text on light background or light text on dark background.
- No "gray on gray."

- If you used colored text, it still reads clearly.

Microsoft notes that the Accessibility Checker can find insufficient color contrast in many text cases, and also explains the value of high-contrast color schemes.

3) Spelling checked

- Run spelling check.
- Check names, places, and key terms manually (spell check does not know every name).

4) Links tested

- Click every hyperlink in Slide Show mode.
- Test action buttons if you used them.

Microsoft explicitly advises testing hyperlinks in Slide Show before presenting.

5) Presenter View tested

If you plan to use Presenter View:

- Turn it on and confirm it shows notes and next slide.
- Confirm which monitor shows Presenter View.

Microsoft explains Presenter View shows current slide, next slide, and speaker notes, and is enabled from Slide Show tab using the "Use Presenter View" checkbox, then choosing the monitor.

6) Media tested (video and audio)

- Play every video.

- Listen for audio level.
- If video is critical, confirm it is .mp4 (H.264 + AAC) or another supported format.

Microsoft recommends .mp4 with H.264 and AAC for best compatibility.

7) File safety

- Save a backup copy.
- Export a PDF copy (for emergencies and printing).
- Copy everything to a USB drive (PPTX and PDF).

Your file's term "Removable media" is relevant here because it is the simplest physical backup method when internet is unreliable.

8) Final flow check (60 seconds)

- Go to Slide Sorter view.
- Confirm the order makes sense.
- Confirm the last slide is the correct ending (summary, call to action, or Q and A).

D) A simple "emergency plan" when things go wrong

Even with preparation, something can still fail. Here is a calm plan you can teach readers:

1. If the file will not open
   Try the backup copy. If still failing, open the PDF version and present from that.

2. If fonts look wrong
   Switch to a common font quickly and continue.

Missing fonts cause substitution on other computers.

3. If video fails
Explain the idea without the video, show a screenshot, and continue. Convert to the recommended format later.

4. If the file is too big to share
Use PowerPoint's file-size reduction options (discard editing data, compress images, lower resolution, embed fewer font characters).

5. If links fail
Navigate manually using Slide Sorter or slide thumbnails. Links must be tested in Slide Show before presenting.

That emergency plan is not about being perfect. It is about staying in control.

E) The "one skill" that makes troubleshooting easier

If you want one skill that makes all fixes faster, it is this:

Know what you selected.

Your book explains that special formatting tools appear in the Format tab when you select a picture or object. If you click the slide background by mistake, those tools disappear, and beginners assume PowerPoint removed them.

So train yourself and your readers to do this:

- Click the object.
- Look at the Ribbon.

- Use the contextual tab that appears.

That habit removes confusion and saves time across every chapter.

FINAL NOTICE TO THE READER

Thank you for finishing this book.

If you are reading this page, it means you did more than "learn about PowerPoint." You practiced. You tried. You made mistakes. You fixed them. That is how real skill is built.

PowerPoint is not only a school tool or an office tool. It is a communication tool. When you learn it, you learn how to take an idea from your mind and place it clearly in front of other people. That ability can help you in school, work, ministry, training, business, and even family responsibilities where you must explain plans and decisions.

Before you close this book, keep these final reminders:

- Practice beats talent. A simple deck made weekly will teach you faster than a perfect deck made once.

- Slides support the speaker. Do not turn slides into your full speech. Use speaker notes for your words.

- Clean beats clever. Clear fonts, simple layouts, and strong spacing often win over heavy design.

- Test before you present. Most presentation failures happen because the deck was not tested on the actual computer, screen, or projector.

- Keep backups. Save your PPTX and export a PDF. Carry both when the presentation matters.

One more thing: PowerPoint versions can look slightly different from computer to computer. Buttons may move, names may change, and some tools may appear in different places. Do not let that discourage you. The skills stay the same. If you understand the basics in this book, you can adjust to any version.

Now take the next step.

Build one real presentation this week, even if it is only 6 slides. Make it for something you already understand. Teach a lesson. Share a report. Present a plan. Tell a story. Then improve the next one.

You are ready.

COPIES, PERMISSIONS, AND TRAINING USE

Copyright © 2026 John Monyjok Maluth. All rights reserved.

No part of this book may be reproduced, stored, or transmitted in any form or by any means, whether electronic, mechanical, photocopying, recording, scanning, or otherwise, without written permission from the author, except for brief quotations used in reviews and educational references.

Personal use allowance:

- You may print a small portion for personal study and private practice.
- You may create your own practice files based on the exercises in this book.

Training, classroom, and bulk copies:
If you want to use this book for a school program, church training, staff development, workshops, or group study, you are welcome to request permission and bulk pricing.

FOR PERMISSIONS, BULK ORDERS, AND TRAINING USE, CONTACT:

John Monyjok Maluth
Website: www.johnshalom.com
Email: maluthabiel@gmail.com
Phone: +211 927 145 394

ABOUT THE AUTHOR

John Monyjok Maluth is a writer, teacher, and practical technology trainer. He works with real learners in real settings, including places where time is limited, internet is unstable, and the need for clear communication is high.

His approach to computer training is simple: teach what people actually use, explain it in plain language, and build skill through practice projects, not theory.

John writes to empower beginners, especially students, staff, ministry teams, and everyday users who want to create presentations that look clean, speak clearly, and work reliably on any computer.

You can reach him through:

Website: www.johnshalom.com
Email: maluthabiel@gmail.com
Phone: +211 927 145 394

www.ingramcontent.com/pod-product-compliance
Lightning Source LLC
Chambersburg PA
CBHW020900180526
45163CB00007B/2567